MIRO
IN THE COLLECTION OF
THE MUSEUM OF MODERN ART

MIRO

IN THE COLLECTION OF
THE MUSEUM OF MODERN ART

including remainder-interest and promised gifts

WILLIAM RUBIN

Distributed by New York Graphic Society Ltd., Greenwich, Connecticut

THE MUSEUM OF MODERN ART, NEW YORK

frontispiece: Miró at Pierre Loeb's, Paris, 1935 or 1936

CONTENTS

LIST OF ILLUSTRATIONS

PREFACE

This book, issued in honor of Joan Miró's eightieth birthday, continues the program of documenting the Museum's painting and sculpture collection. The works recorded and illustrated here are either already at the Museum or fall into the categories of remainder-interest gifts (works that are the property of the institution but remain with the donors for their lifetime) or promised gifts (works that have been formally committed as future gifts or bequests). The entire group, which contains a number of Miró's unrivaled masterpieces, constitutes the finest and most complete collection of his art in public or private hands.

The formation of this group of forty paintings, sculptures, and collages was achieved through the efforts of many curators and the generosity of many trustees and friends of the Museum Collections. Foremost among these was Alfred H. Barr, Jr., first Director of the Museum, and later, until his retirement in 1967, Director of the Museum Collections. Especially identified with the Miró collection has been the painter's long-time friend James Thrall Soby, whose classic monograph was published in conjunction with the Museum's large Miró retrospective of 1959. From 1943 to 1945 Director of Painting and Sculpture and for many years thereafter Chairman of the Department of Painting and Sculpture Exhibitions, Mr. Soby was instrumental in acquiring a number of Mirós and is himself the donor of four important works. James Johnson Sweeney, also a friend of Miró and writer on his art, directed the Museum's first Miró retrospective in 1941–42. During his brief tenure as Director of Painting and Sculpture (1945–46) the Museum acquired two of its most important Miró paintings.

Last, but far from least, has been the generosity of the artist himself in giving of both his work and his time. The artist has donated outright a large painting and an object-sculpture, as well as twelve important drawings and a collage that constitute the preparatory studies for three of the key paintings in the Museum Collection. In addition, he contributed substantially toward the acquisition of the monumental bronze *Moonbird* (p. 99), and himself contributed two works to be sold in order to raise funds for the purchase of *The Birth of the World* (p. 31). During the preparation of this book Miró has given unstintingly of

his time; he has freely discussed the techniques and iconography of his works and graciously allowed me to take notes during our numerous discussions. (In the following commentaries all the direct and indirect quotations from Miró for which sources are not indicated come from my interviews with the artist.) Indeed, it is this cooperation by Miró that has made possible the present publication of the first thoroughgoing analyses of many of his works in the Museum's collection.

The first Mirós to enter the Museum Collection were purchased from among the works being assembled for the pioneering exhibition, presented by Alfred Barr, "Fantastic Art, Dada, Surrealism," December 7, 1936, to January 17, 1937. The *Cadavre exquis* (p. 35), the very first, was acquired late in 1935 while preparations for the show were under way. Early the next year *The Hunter (Catalan Landscape)* (p. 23) was purchased, and *Rope and People I* (p. 69) was received as a gift from the Pierre Matisse Gallery.

In 1937, Mr. Barr negotiated the purchase of *Person Throwing a Stone at a Bird* (cover and p. 36), which had also figured in "Fantastic Art, Dada, Surrealism," from the distinguished Belgian collector René Gaffé. It was from the widow of this pioneer Miró collector that the Museum was later to acquire the monumental *Birth of the World*. In fact, the Gaffé collection has been the source of a number of the Museum's important paintings, including Chagall's *I and the Village* and Roger de La Fresnaye's *The Conquest of the Air*. Also in 1937, Mr. Barr purchased through Paul Eluard, from the collection of André Breton, the *Relief Construction* (p. 53) which had figured not only in "Fantastic Art, Dada, Surrealism," but also in the earlier exhibition "Cubism and Abstract Art," March 2 to April 19, 1936. In the summer of 1937, when Mr. Barr and members of the acquisitions committee were in Europe, they chose from the Galerie Pierre in Paris a large Miró, which was subsequently exchanged for an even finer one, *Painting*, 1933 (p. 59), in the collection of the chairman of the committee, the painter George L. K. Morris.

In 1945, while Mr. Sweeney was Director of Painting and Sculpture, the collection obtained two of its crucial works, *Dutch Interior I* (p. 42), acquired through the Mrs. Simon Guggenheim Fund, and *The Beautiful Bird Revealing the Unknown to a Pair of Lovers* (p. 80), paid for with funds from the sale of work from the Lillie P. Bliss Bequest.

For a decade following the end of World War II no new Mirós entered the Painting and Sculpture Collection. Then, in 1955, Armand G. Erpf provided funds to acquire *Table with Glove* (p. 17), one of the key works of the early "realist" period. A year later, Nelson A. Rockefeller, who in 1958 was to make a promised gift of the extraordinary *Hirondelle / Amour* (p. 65), gave an unusual collage (p. 63). Mr. Rockefeller's promised gift was occasioned by the exhibition "Works of Art: Given and Promised." The same 1958 exhibition contained *Still Life with Old Shoe* (p. 73) and *Self-Portrait I* (p. 77), two entirely unique Mirós promised by James Thrall Soby; three years later, Mr. Soby was to add *Portrait of Mistress Mills in 1750* (p. 48) and *Collage, 1934* (p. 66), to the list of Mirós with the promise of the future bequest of his entire collection.

During the last decade and a half the Miró collection has more than doubled; virtually every year has brought new acquisitions in the form of gifts and purchases. The year 1961 saw the gift by Mr. and Mrs. Jan Mitchell of *The Family* (p. 29), one of Miró's most elaborate and extraordinary drawings, as well as the donation of *Object* (p. 55), a Surrealist construction, by Mr. and Mrs. Harold X. Weinstein. The Kay Sage Tanguy Bequest, which came to the Museum two years later, contained an important Miró collage, and Mrs. Simon Guggenheim consented to have her fund used for the magnificent *Mural Painting* (p. 86), originally executed by Miró for Harvard University.

In 1964 William H. Weintraub gave the pastel *Opera Singer* (p. 68), the first of two important Mirós he and his wife were to donate, and the next year Pierre Matisse presented the Museum with *Object* (p. 71), the most extraordinary of Miró's Surrealist constructions, and the second of Mr. Matisse's three Miró gifts. The last Miró acquired under the stewardship of Mr. Barr, *Person, Woman, Bird, Star at Sunset* (p. 93), was purchased at auction from the G. David Thompson Collection through the Kay Sage Tanguy Fund.

In 1968 an important *Collage* of 1929 (p. 51) was purchased through the James Thrall Soby Fund, and the following year Mr. and Mrs. Edwin A. Bergman made a promised gift of *Personage* (p. 90), the first of Miró's ceramic sculptures destined for the Collection. Also in 1969, Mr. and Mrs. William H. Weintraub gave the large and important *Seated Woman I* (p. 79).

In 1970, the Museum was able to purchase the large and unusual *Song of the Vowels* (p. 97) with monies from the Mrs. Simon Guggenheim Fund that the late Mrs. Guggenheim contributed especially in honor of Dorothy C. Miller, then retiring as Senior Curator of the Department of Painting and Sculpture. In the same year the monumental sculpture *Moonbird* (p. 99) was also acquired.

Last year, Pierre Matisse donated the third of his Miró gifts, the unique *Portrait of a Man in a Late Nineteenth Century Frame* (p. 84). The Museum was also able to conclude the purchase, hoped for since 1969, of *The Birth of the World* (p. 31), with the assistance of the artist himself, an anonymous fund, the Armand G. Erpf Fund, and the Mr. and Mrs. Joseph Slifka Fund. The year 1972 also saw the commitment by an anonymous donor of three much-needed works: *Collage, 1933* (p. 61), *Head of a Man* (p. 75), and the ceramic *Head* (p. 91).

Early this year, Miró made the gifts referred to above: the painting *Woman with Three Hairs Surrounded by Birds in the Night* (p. 103) given in honor of James Thrall Soby; the object-sculpture *Personnage au parapluie* (p. 54); the particular colored postcard on which *Dutch Interior I* was based, as well as the seven studies that mediate between them; a reproduction of the engraving upon which *Portrait of Mistress Mills in 1750* is based, as well as the four studies for the latter picture; and finally the large *Collage* (p. 58), which served as the point of departure for *Painting, 1933*.

Shortly after receiving Miró's gifts, the Museum was able to announce the promised gift of the *Bather* (p. 57) by Mr. and Mrs. Armand Bartos and a few months later the extraordinary promise of gifts of five Mirós from the collection of Mr. and Mrs. Gordon Bunshaft: the large *Landscape* (p. 39), *Gouache-Drawing* (p. 67), *Painting* (p. 83), the sculpture *Personage and Bird* (p. 101), and the "tapestry" *Sobreteixim 5* (p. 104), which brings the Museum's representation of Miró's work up to 1972. All these promised gifts give superb representation of periods and types of Miró's work otherwise not well—or not at all—represented in the Collection.

IN THIS BOOK, the notes and the reference photographs for each work appear under the full catalog entry in the back of the volume. The page number of that full entry is given at the end of the short caption that accompanies the reproduction of each work.

The preparation of this catalog and of the exhibition for which it serves has involved the efforts of a great many people. Beyond the artist himself I owe special thanks to his friend and dealer, Pierre Matisse, and to Jacques Dupin, of the Galerie Maeght, author of the definitive monograph on Miró's work. Margit Rowell, Associate Curator of the Guggenheim Museum, graciously consented to read the manuscript and made numerous helpful suggestions. Professor Christian Tual has generously made available to me the text of an important unpublished letter from Miró to M. Tual's father.

Carolyn Lanchner, Researcher of the Collection, made enormous contributions to this book. She has participated significantly in every way; I think of her as almost my coauthor. Francis Kloeppel, editor of the volume, has made many excellent suggestions and has been a great pleasure to work with.

My special thanks to Carl Laanes who, in the designing of this book, worked out a number of knotty problems; Jack Doenias has cheerfully overseen production; Inga Forslund has prepared the list of publications, and Linda Creigh has good-naturedly undertaken much of the typing. Frances Keech took on the task of securing permission to reproduce the many reference photographs. Nancy Karumba, Curatorial Assistant in the Department of Painting and Sculpture, has been invaluable in the preparation of the exhibition for which this book serves as catalog.

Finally, a word in praise of my hard-working assistant, Judith di Meo, whose collaboration at every stage has made what might have been a chore a pleasure.

William Rubin
May 1973

Miró in 1931, Rue François Mouthon, Paris
Miró in his studio, c. 1956

9

EXHIBITIONS OF MIRO'S WORK

AT THE MUSEUM OF MODERN ART

THIS LIST INCLUDES all one-man exhibitions of Miró at The Museum of Modern Art, as well as others in which a significant number of his works were included.

"Painting in Paris," January 19–February 16, 1930. 2 works. Directed by Alfred H. Barr, Jr.

"Modern Works of Art: 5th Anniversary Exhibition," November 20, 1934–January 20, 1935. 1 work. Directed by Alfred H. Barr, Jr.

"Cubism and Abstract Art," March 2–April 19, 1936. 5 works. Directed by Alfred H. Barr, Jr.

"Fantastic Art, Dada, Surrealism," December 7, 1936–January 17, 1937. 15 works. Directed by Alfred H. Barr, Jr.

"Twelve Modern Paintings," April 28–May 30, 1937. 5 works. Directed by Alfred H. Barr, Jr.

"Art in Our Time: 10th Anniversary Exhibition," May 10–September 30, 1939. 2 works. Painting and sculpture section directed by Alfred H. Barr, Jr.

"Modern Masters from European and American Collections," January 26–May 24, 1940. 1 work. Directed by Dorothy C. Miller.

"Joan Miró," November 19, 1941–January 11, 1942. 73 works. Directed by James Johnson Sweeney.

"Modern Drawings," February 16–May 10, 1944. 3 works. Directed by Monroe Wheeler.

"Art in Progress: 15th Anniversary Exhibition," May 24–October 15, 1944. 2 works. Painting and Sculpture Section directed by James Thrall Soby.

"Miró Mural," March 2–April 4, 1948. Installed by Alfred H. Barr, Jr.

"Paintings from the Museum Collection: 25th Anniversary Exhibition," October 19, 1954–January 2, 1955. 10 works. Installed by Alfred H. Barr, Jr., and Dorothy C. Miller.

"Paintings from Private Collections: A 25th Anniversary Exhibition," May 31–September 5, 1955. 6 works. Directed by Alfred H. Barr, Jr.

"Works of Art: Given or Promised," October 8–November 9, 1958. 2 works. Directed by Alfred H. Barr, Jr.

"Joan Miró," March 18–May 10, 1959. 122 works. Directed by William S. Lieberman.

"The Art of Assemblage," October 2–November 12, 1961. 3 works. Directed by William C. Seitz.

"The School of Paris: Paintings from the Florene May Shoenborn and Samuel A. Marx Collection," November 2, 1965–January 2, 1966. 4 works. Directed by Monroe Wheeler, installed by Alicia Legg.

"Dada, Surrealism, and Their Heritage," March 27–June 9, 1968. 24 works. Directed by William Rubin.

"Twentieth-Century Art from the Nelson Aldrich Rockefeller Collection," May 26–September 1, 1969. 5 works. Directed by Dorothy C. Miller.

"Miró Prints," March 9–May 11, 1970. 54 works. Directed by Riva Castleman.

"Philadelphia in New York: 90 Modern Works from the Philadelphia Museum of Art," October 18, 1972–January 7, 1973. 6 works. Directed by Betsy Jones.

"Joan Miró," November 19, 1941–January 11, 1942
"Joan Miró," March 18–May 10, 1959

"Joan Miró," March 18–May 10, 1959
"Miró Prints," March 9–May 11, 1970

PUBLICATIONS ON MIRO
Issued by The Museum of Modern Art

Monographs

Joan Miró. By James Johnson Sweeney. 1941. 87 pp. incl. 70 ills. (4 col.), portrait.

Includes catalog of the exhibition, November 18, 1941–January 11, 1942. Chronology, works by Miró in American museums, list of exhibitions, prints by Miró, books illustrated by Miró, ballets in which Miró collaborated, and bibliography.

Reprint edition by Arno Press, New York, 1969. (All ills. in black and white.)

Joan Miró. By James Thrall Soby. 1959. 164 pp. incl. 148 ills. (35 col.), portrait.

Published in connection with the exhibition, March 18–May 10, 1959. Includes list of exhibitions and bibliography. Book jacket design by Miró.

Also Spanish edition, 1960.

Separate catalog of the exhibition published. [8] pp. Also shown at the Los Angeles County Museum, June 10–July 21, 1959, for which slightly different catalog was issued. [8] pp.

General Books and Exhibition Catalogs

Painting in Paris from American Collections. Edited by Alfred H. Barr, Jr. 1930. p. 35. 1 ill. of Miró's work.

Catalog of exhibition, January 19–February 16, 1930.

Modern Works of Art. Fifth anniversary exhibition. Edited by Alfred H. Barr, Jr. 1934. pp. 31–32. 1 ill. of Miró's work.

Catalog of exhibition, November 20, 1934–January 20, 1935.

Cubism and Abstract Art. By Alfred H. Barr, Jr. 1936. pp. 180–85, 217. 3 ills. of Miró's work.

Includes catalog of exhibition, March 2–April 19, 1936. Reprint edition by Arno Press, New York, 1966.

Fantastic Art, Dada, Surrealism. Edited by Alfred H. Barr, Jr. 1936. p. 227 and passim. 6 ills. of Miró's work.

Includes catalog of exhibition, December 7, 1936–January 17, 1937.

Second revised edition, 1937, and third revised edition, 1947, contain essays by Georges Hugnet.

Art in Our Time. An exhibition to celebrate the tenth anniversary of The Museum of Modern Art and the opening of its new building, held at the time of the New York World's Fair. 1939. plate 196. 1 ill. of Miró's work.

Catalog of exhibition, May 10–September 30, 1939.

Modern Masters from European and American Collections. 1940. p. 32. 1 ill. of Miró's work.

Catalog of exhibition, January 26–March 24, 1940.

Painting and Sculpture in The Museum of Modern Art. Edited by Alfred H. Barr, Jr. 1942. p. 61. 2 ills. of Miró's work.

Supplement edited by James Johnson Sweeney. 1945. p. 11. 1 ill. of Miró's work.

———— ————. 1948. pp. 126, 215–18, 278. 8 ills. of Miró's work.

———— ————. 1958. p. 43.

The above catalogs of the Museum's collection are supplemented by publications entitled "Painting and Sculpture Acquisitions," which appeared as Bulletins at various intervals.

20th Century Portraits. By Monroe Wheeler. 1942. pp. 19, 102. 1 ill. of Miró's work.

Includes catalog of exhibition, December 9, 1942–January 24, 1943.

What Is Modern Painting? By Alfred H. Barr, Jr. 1943. p. 33. 1 ill. of Miró's work. (Introductory Series to the Modern Arts. 2.)

Last revised edition (7th), 1959. Also editions in Spanish and Portuguese, 1953.

Modern Drawings. Edited by Monroe Wheeler. 1944. pp. 13, 14, 76. 1 ill. of Miró's work.

Includes catalog of exhibition, February 16–May 10, 1944.

Second revised edition, 1945. Third revised edition, 1947.

Art in Progress. A survey prepared for the fifteenth anniversary of The Museum of Modern Art, New York. 1944. pp. 93, 195, 222. 1 ill. of Miró's work.

Includes catalog of exhibition, May 24–October 22, 1944.

Contemporary Painters. By James Thrall Soby. 1948. pp. 99–103: "Three Humorists: Klee, Miró, Calder." 1 ill. of Miró's work.

Modern Art in Your Life. By Robert Goldwater in collaboration with René d'Harnoncourt. 1949. pp. 28, 30–31. 2 ills. of Miró's work.

Includes catalog of exhibition, October 5–December 4, 1949. Published as *The Museum of Modern Art Bulletin*, v. 17, no. 1, 1949.

Second revised edition, 1953.

Modern Art, Old and New. By René d'Harnoncourt. 1950. plate 34. 1 ill. of Miró's work. (Teaching Portfolio. 3.)

A portfolio based on the exhibition "Timeless Aspects of Modern Art," held at The Museum of Modern Art, New York, November 16, 1948–January 23, 1949.

Masters of Modern Art. Edited by Alfred H. Barr, Jr. 1954. pp. 142, 143, 228. 3 col. ills. of Miró's work.

Second edition, 1955. Also foreign-language editions (French, Spanish, 1955; German, Swedish, 1956).

Paintings from Private Collections. A 25th anniversary exhibition of The Museum of Modern Art, New York. 1955. pp. 15, 16, 23.

Catalog of exhibition, May 31–September 5, 1955.

Supplemented by *The Museum of Modern Art Bulletin,* v. 22, no. 4, Summer 1955. pp. [27, 28]. 6 ills. of Miró's work.

Works of Art: Given or Promised. 1958. pp. 30, 31. 2 ills. of Miró's work.

Catalog of exhibition, October 8–November 9, 1958.

Published as *The Museum of Modern Art Bulletin,* v. 26, no. 1, Fall 1958, together with the catalog of the exhibition of The Philip L. Goodwin Collection, shown simultaneously.

The James Thrall Soby Collection of Works of Art Pledged or Given to The Museum of Modern Art. 1961. pp. 56–59. 3 ills. of Miró's work.

Catalog of exhibition at M. Knoedler and Company, Inc., New York, February 1–25 (extended to March 4). Catalog with notes by James Thrall Soby. Preface by Blanchette H. Rockefeller. "James Thrall Soby and His Collection" by Alfred H. Barr, Jr.

The Art of Assemblage. By William C. Seitz. 1961. pp. 25, 39, 62, 63, 65, 72, 73. 3 ills. of Miró's work.

Includes catalog of exhibition, October 4–November 12, 1961.

Published in collaboration with The Dallas Museum for Contemporary Arts and the San Francisco Museum of Art.

The School of Paris. Paintings from the Florene May Schoenborn and Samuel A. Marx Collection. 1965. pp. 46–49. 4 ills. (1 col.) of Miró's work.

Catalog of exhibition, November 2, 1965–January 2, 1966. Preface by Alfred H. Barr, Jr. Introduction by James Thrall Soby. Notes by Lucy R. Lippard.

All paintings in the collection reproduced.

Published in collaboration with The Art Institute of Chicago, City Art Museum of St. Louis, San Francisco Museum of Art, Museo de Arte Moderno, Mexico City.

Dada, Surrealism, and Their Heritage. By William S. Rubin. 1968. pp. 64–72, 131–35, and passim. 22 ills. (1 col.) of Miró's work.

Includes catalog of exhibition, March 27–June 9, 1968.

De Cézanne a Miró. 1968. pp. 55, 61. 2 ills. (1 col.) of Miró's work.

Catalog of circulating exhibition, organized under the auspices of the International Council of The Museum of Modern Art, New York. Preface by Mrs. Donald B. Straus. Introduction by Monroe Wheeler. Text in Spanish.

Shown in Museo Nacional de Bellas Artes, Buenos Aires, May 15–June 5, 1968; Museo de Arte Contemporáneo de la Universidad de Chile, Santiago, June 26–July 17; Museo de Bellas Artes, Caracas, August 4–25; Center for Inter-American Relations, New York, September 12–22.

Twentieth-Century Art from the Nelson Aldrich Rockefeller Collection. 1969. pp. 24, 79–81. 3 ills. (1 col.) of Miró's work.

Foreword by Monroe Wheeler. Preface by Nelson A. Rockefeller. "The Nelson Aldrich Rockefeller Collection" by William S. Lieberman, pp. 11–35.

Includes catalog of exhibition, May 26–September 1, 1969.

Joan Miró. Fifty Recent Prints. 1969. [6] pp. incl. 6 ills. (1 col.)

Catalog of exhibition, March 9–May 11, 1970. Text by Riva Castleman.

An Invitation to See. 125 paintings from The Museum of Modern Art. Introduction and comments by Helen M. Franc. 1973. pp. 72, 89, 90. 3 col. ills. of Miró's work.

(Compiled by Inga Forslund, Associate Librarian)

MIRO
IN THE COLLECTION OF
THE MUSEUM OF MODERN ART

TABLE WITH GLOVE. *Paris, winter 1921. Oil on canvas, 46 x 35¼ inches. (Full Catalog entry and Notes, p. 109)*

During much of his career, Miró's painting has oscillated between the ornamental and the spare, configurations that in his work tend to induce their opposites. In these terms the almost primitive simplicity of the Museum's *Table with Glove*, executed in 1921, may be viewed as a response to *The Table* (fig. 1), his most important prolix composition of the previous year.

If the suave ornamentation of *The Table* is not to be found in *Table with Glove*, neither are the allusions to Cubist structure. Although the composition is likewise iconically frontal, and the tabletop is similarly tilted toward the picture plane, the effect here much less recalls Cubism (or antecedents in Cézanne) than it does naïf art — and doubtless Miró's keen appreciation of the Douanier Rousseau. The contours of the pitcher, cane, glove, and folio of drawings are generally much simpler and more summary than those of the motifs in *The Table*, and the uncovered part of the tabletop is treated as a bold, flat plane. Indeed, the conscious "awkwardness" of Miró's drawing here — especially in the contouring of the glove and the rim of the tabletop — proposes a spirit of provincial stiffness and sincerity. This sobriety, which Miró no doubt felt as antidotal to the exuberance of *The Table*, would lead to greater simplification later in 1921 in the schematic reductions of *Standing Nude* (fig. 2).

Miró's choice in this picture of an almost rustic table on a simple support — as against the Baroque hyperbole of the furniture in *The Table* — is entirely in keeping with his shift in taste in 1921. To be sure, this particular table and pitcher were among the furnishings of Pablo Gargallo's studio in the Rue Blomet that Miró was subletting at the time.[1] The cane and portfolio belonged to Miró, as did the fur-lined glove that the artist recalls needing because the studio was so cold. Miró says he put the glove in the painting because it was so stiff that it had retained the shape of his hand.[2] Indeed, schematized surrogates for Miró's hand — and his eye — were to become the most frequent symbols of his improvisational paintings four years later.

The flat-footed, intentionally obvious composition of *Table with Glove* — the parallelisms between the cane and portfolio and the tablelegs, the disposition of the objects around the center of the circular tabletop — suggests a "primitiveness" that belies the complex configurations of the still lifes of the previous year.[3] This goes hand in hand with a much greater flatness than before, for which achievement — so crucial to his later art — Miró felt the need of momentarily discarding other compositional baggage. Likewise, the decorative, quasi-Fauve palette of 1920 gives way here to sober browns, ochers, and dull orange, relieved only by the saturated accents of red, mauve, and green in the cock inscribed on the pitcher and the dotted pattern of the portfolio. The intricate patterning of the cock and the almost Art Nouveau elegance of the ribbon bows serve as grace notes for the sober line of the composition.

While the cost of *Table with Glove*'s austerity is the loss of much that fascinates us in Miró's color and drawing of the years just preceding, there is nevertheless a great gain in the direction of monumentality. The motifs, whose flattened forms reach out to touch the edges of the pictorial field, locking the configuration to the frame, seem larger than life. Here Miró presents fewer objects than in *The Table*, and shows them bigger, closer up. The effect makes the composition loom into the picture plane in a manner anticipating the immense *personnages* of Miró's later style (p. 103).

THE CARBIDE LAMP. *Montroig, Paris, 1922–23. Oil on canvas, 15 x 18 inches. (C&N, p. 110)*

During 1921–22 Miró encapsulated virtually the whole of his vision of rural Catalonia in one painting, the celebrated *Farm* (fig. 3), an image of the family home at Montroig[1]—a place so vital to him that he has returned there every summer, whether from Paris, Barcelona, or, more recently, Palma. *The Farm* at once subsumed and extrapolated the motifs of Miró's landscapes of the five years preceding its execution. It also represented the epitome of his "detailistic"[2] realism; the myriad, mostly small motifs which spot its surface are fastidiously executed, and the whole shimmers with an ornamentalism beyond that of his previous paintings.

The Farm required immense effort and concentration. Miró speaks of feeling entirely drained, indeed a bit lost, after its completion. A few months later, during the summer in Montroig, he began to dispel this sense of crisis by starting five pictures, all but one of them small-format still lifes, which were to be finished in Paris during the following autumn and winter. Of these, the Museum's *Carbide Lamp*, its *Ear of Grain*, and the *Grill and Carbide Lamp* (fig. 4) constitute a trio in their identity of size, character, and palette, and may be thought of as a coda to *The Farm*, inasmuch as the still-life motifs look as though they might have been excerpted from the larger picture. At the same time, Miró's anti-anecdotal isolation of these objects in the fields of the new pictures and the rigorous, ascetic geometries of their compositions constitute an antithesis to the prolixity of *The Farm*.

This "focusing down" on a few humble objects was Miró's way of finding himself again. (He was to do much

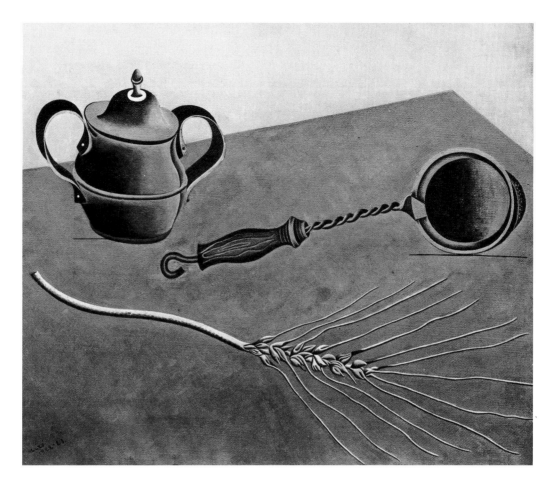

THE EAR OF GRAIN. *Montroig, Paris, 1922–23. Oil on canvas, 14⅞ x 18⅛ inches. (C&N, p. 111)*

the same thing early in 1937 when a temporary crisis led him to paint *Still Life with Old Shoe,* p. 73.) From Montroig, he wrote his friend Roland Tual: [3]

The effort of my last picture [The Farm] does not permit me to undertake comparable subjects. I search the kitchen for humble objects, ordinary objects—an ear of grain, a grill[4]—from which I make a picture. To communicate emotion through objects you must love them immensely because you may be sure that in the contrary case you will make a picture wholly without interest. I become more demanding of myself from day to day, an exigency which makes me rework a picture if one of its elements is a millimeter too much to the right or left. In the room which serves as my atelier I always have books that I read during the intervals in my work. All this requires a continual sense of spiritual vibration. When I paint, I caress what I am making, and the effort to endow it with a meaningful life tires me enormously. Sometimes, after a session of work, I fall into an armchair, exhausted, as after the act of lovemaking.[5]

The crystalline surfaces of *The Carbide Lamp* and *Ear of Grain* do not at all betray the intense labor of Miró's continual reworking as he brought the compositions into adjustment—he has spoken of the "especially rigorous discipline" of that summer. Of the two, *The Ear of Grain* is the more conventional in the spatial disposition of its forms, and it is the more easily interpreted. The shapes of the crockery jar, the strainer, and the ear of grain splay rightward from the left of the canvas, the downward diagonal of the grain counterbalanced by the upward movement of the contour of the gray tabletop. In variance with the tilting of the latter, the jar is seen from a position only slightly above profile, while the strainer is pictured entirely from above—a series of perspective disjunctions by then long sanctioned by the Cubists. Nevertheless, Miró inserted "ground lines" under the bowl and at the bottom edge of the strainer, as if he felt the need to clarify their disposition in space.

The motifs in *The Carbide Lamp* are more disjoined, more contradictory in position and scale than those of *The Ear of Grain*. The lamp itself—there was no electricity then in Montroig—sits on a trapezoid of ocher which Miró introduced "to keep equilibrium," and which might be read as a stylized symbol of cast light. This ocher shape is itself set in a field of gray that we take to be the tabletop but which is now identical with the picture field itself and thus entirely vertical. The tomato in the lower left corner has been halved vertically to reiterate the line of the frame, already echoed by the left contour of the trapezoid; it has also been sectioned laterally to reveal its interior, whose ornamental stylization provides a foil for the austerity of the picture as a whole. On the right, tilted at a distorting angle, and immensely enlarged to provide dramatic diagonal accents, is a metal stand for a clothes iron.

The objects in *The Carbide Lamp* are conventional in themselves; they do not interact to release those mysterious poetic signals which, under the influence of Surrealism, Miró's iconography would later give off. Yet there *is* a sense of mystery in the structural disjunctions and juxtapositions of their forms, and it is perhaps this which Picasso—an early admirer of Miró's art—had in mind when he characterized the picture as "poetry."[6]

While the structural severity of *The Carbide Lamp* would have been inconceivable without Cubism, the picture has little resemblance to the work of Picasso or Braque—or even Gris, with whose work its chaste, metallic coloring has some affinity. Superb and concentrated as this small composition is, its type of sober geometricity was not at the center of Miró's genius, and he was not to press further in this direction. Indeed, not long after he completed these still lifes, *Ear of Grain* in the hotel room he had taken on the Boulevard Raspail and *Carbide Lamp* in a boardinghouse on the Rue Berthollet,[7] Miró departed suddenly and radically toward the realization of his mature style in *The Tilled Field* (fig. 5).

THE HUNTER (CATALAN LANDSCAPE). *Montroig, Paris, 1923–24. Oil on canvas, 25½ x 39½ inches. (C&N, p. 111)*

The Hunter, also known as *Catalan Landscape*,[1] is Miró's first painting realized wholly within the profile of his personal style, the first free of the manifest influences of Cubism and Fauvism. Its gracile drawing, which links the entire surface in its filigree tracery, is of a tenuousness that remains unsurpassed in his work. And its imagery witnesses the introduction of many signs and symbols that were to become familiar in the landscape of *miromonde*.

The still lifes that Miró completed during his sojourn in Paris in the winter of 1922–23 (discussed on pages 18–19) mark the conclusion of his realism as such.[2] That winter had been noteworthy for his intense involvement with poetry and with the theories propagated by the nascent Surrealist movement; during Miró's entire stay in Paris from the autumn of 1922 until the spring of the following year he started no new paintings, contenting himself with the completion of the small canvases begun the previous summer at Montroig. Miró had already been on familiar terms with many of the younger avant-garde poets,[3] and was, as we have seen, a voracious reader. But now, partly through his friendship with André Masson, this literary passion was to dominate his time.

Such were Miró's concerns as he left for Montroig early in the summer of 1923. The painter, who had earlier brought actual grass from Montroig to Paris to guarantee the realism of *The Farm*, "now carried to Montroig the seeds of rebellion, humor, and the fantastic that he had found in Paris. They would soon germinate, grow and bear their first fruit . . . In all the feverish activity of the Rue Blomet they could never have grown hardily. They needed the more natural forcing bed of the Catalan earth."[4] Indeed, it is precisely the fusion of cosmopolitan Parisian culture and the Catalan environment—the latter comprehending the region's folk art and craftsmanship, cave paintings, and Romanesque frescoes as well as its characteristic landscape and architecture—that accounts for the unique spirit and flavor of Miró's art. The artist alluded to this combination in declaring that he wanted to "become an international Catalan."[5]

A proper appreciation of the place of *The Hunter* in Miró's development requires some knowledge of *The Tilled Field* (fig. 5), the unique transitional work that separates *The Hunter* from the still lifes of 1922–23 discussed above. Usually an artist arrives at his mature style through an evolution observable within a series of works. Miró's change between these pictures was abrupt because it was profoundly influenced by concerns of an extrapictorial nature.

The Tilled Field, the first step in Miró's plan to "go beyond the *plastique cubiste* to attain poetry," represents in effect a re-creation of the realistic (if highly stylized) *Farm* as modified by the mind's eye. The artist's earlier need to bring grass from Montroig to Paris to complete *The Farm* reflected his then obsession with external reality; now he was working entirely indoors, without direct reference to the motif, distilling its essence, as it were, in the imagination. While at work on *The Tilled Field* and *The Hunter* Miró wrote his friend Ràfols: "I have managed to escape into the absolute of nature, and my landscapes have nothing in common any more with outside reality. Nevertheless they are more 'Montroig' than if they had been done from nature." [6]

The Tilled Field was also Miró's first resolutely "flat" painting, going far beyond *Still Life with Glove* in this regard. Such spatial implications as follow automatically from its horizon line were counteracted by the diagonal that traverses earth and sky on the right and effectively locks both areas into the picture plane; modeling is used only sparsely, and then simply to produce slight indications of relief whose effect is decorative rather than structural. Nevertheless, the geometricized fields against which the smaller curvilinear forms are set—indeed, the very disposition of these masses—as well as the evenly painted color areas, still manifest a debt to Cubism (here of the Synthetic variety). This Cubism was to disappear in *The Hunter* and subsequent pictures as Miró's language became more personal; but its vestiges were less expunged than telescoped into the infrastructure of his compositions.

Although the giant ear, eye, and certain other forms in *The Tilled Field* constitute the first appearance of Miró's subsequently characteristic biomorphism,[7] the picture's originality does not lie primarily in its formal structure. What is most interesting are the fantastical juxtapositions in its imagery: the tree sprouting a frontal eye and profile ear; the lizard in a dunce cap.[8] It was inevitable that this new collage-influenced imagery, which was directly indebted to the principles underlying the poetry and painting of interest to the Surrealists,[9] should have elicited a new manner of painting. This, precisely, is what is con-

summated in *The Hunter*, where Miró's airy, meandering line—a type of draftsmanship that responds to the wandering inflections of thought—serves to string together ideas that are in the nature of "free associations." The resultant tracery implements Miro's avowed goal of making a "pictorial poem"—a type of painting the Surrealists would call *peinture-poésie*.[10]

In *The Hunter* Miró went beyond the stylized realism of *The Tilled Field* by indicating the constituents of his iconography less through representation than through signs and symbols (although he clearly felt no need to adapt the latter to any consistent system). At first glance there appear to be few recognizable motifs in the picture: an eye, an ear, a pipe—and a collection of geometrical forms. Nevertheless, an image of a peasant hunting in the Catalan countryside is indicated with a full panoply of anecdotal details (as shown by reference to Miró's iconographical chart),[11] disguised as they may be in the artist's arcane shorthand. The iconographic elaborateness of *The Hunter* is exceeded only by that of *The Harlequin's Carnival*, begun shortly afterward. By the following year, Miró's schemata were already less particularized and less prolix, and by 1930 he had condensed his motifs into a small, more syncopated vocabulary.

Despite the fact that Miró reports having been originally inspired by a particular Catalan peasant, the hunter himself is represented as a largely unindividuated stick figure (16), perhaps suggested by neolithic-type "memory images" [12] but more reminiscent of those common to the art of children. The hunter stands in the upper left of the picture, his head frontal, his legs and feet in profile; he is mustachioed (12), bearded (15), smokes a pipe (13, 14), and wears a *barretina* (9), a Catalan cap of vaguely Phrygian aspect. While his eye (11) is frontal, his ear (10) is in profile, as is common in memory images, where different components of the body are seen from their most easily grasped or recollected point of view, rather than in consistent perspective with one another.

The hunter's heart (17) shoots small flames—the sign, says Miró, for "fervency" [13]—and his sex (24) takes the form of an egg that extrudes delicate hairs. In his right hand he holds a rabbit [14] (23), in his left, a still-smoking gun (20) whose "bullet," or shot (22), lies nearby; strapped to his sleeve is a knife (19). The cone and sphere that stand for the gun and bullet are iterated and reiterated in progressively smaller size on left and right as what Miró calls

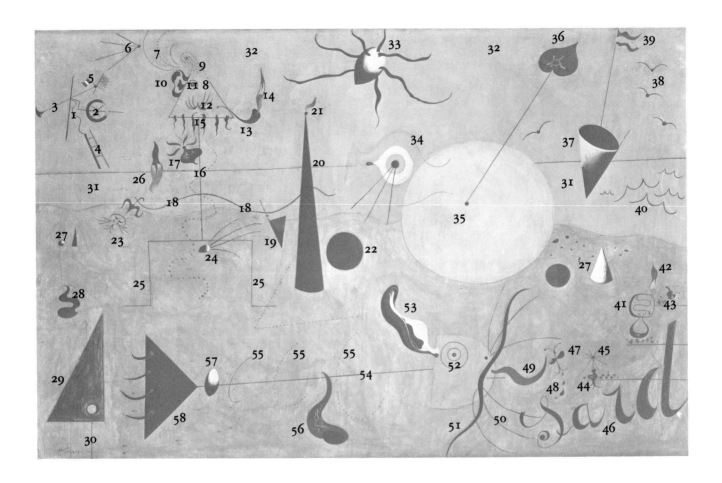

THE HUNTER

1. Bird-airplane
2. Propeller
3. Fuselage
4. Rope ladder
5. French and Catalan flags
6. Star
7. Rainbow
8. Hunter's head
9. Hunter's Catalan cap
10. Hunter's ear
11. Hunter's eye
12. Hunter's moustache
13. Hunter's pipe
14. Smoke
15. Hunter's beard
16. Hunter's body
17. Hunter's heart
18. Hunter's arm

19. Knife
20. Gun
21. Smoke from gun
22. Bullet (shot)
23. Rabbit
24. Hunter's sex organ
25. Hunter's leg
26. Flame
27. Landscape elements
28. Turd
29. Vine
30. Stem
31. Mediterranean Sea
32. Sky
33. Sun-egg
34. Eye
35. Carob tree
36. Carob leaf
37. Small boat
38. Seagulls

39. Spanish flag
40. Waves
41. Grill
42. Hunter's campfire to cook lunch
43. Pepper
44. Potato
45. Potato flower
46. First four letters of word "Sardine"
47. Fly
48. Defecation of fly
49. Sardine's tongue
50. Sardine's whiskers
51. Surface of water
52. Sardine's eye
53. Sardine's ear
54. Sardine's spine
55. Sardine's bones
56. Sardine's bowel
57. Sardine's eggs (reproductive organ)
58. Sardine's tail

"landscape elements" (27). By the same token, the right triangle of the knife is repeated as the "vine" (29) in the lower left corner, a reduction to a geometrical sign of Miró's earlier schematic patterning of a vineyard (fig. 6). Through this reduction of objects into simple signs Miró is able to construct an archetypology of forms whose significances vary with their context; on the one hand such imagistic contraction generates the ambiguity necessary to poetry, and on the other it enhances the possibilities of rhyming, analogizing, inverting, and otherwise playing with the forms in the interest of compositional cohesiveness.

The landscape of *The Hunter* is dominated by a beige circle that stands for the trunk of a large carob tree (35); this tree sprouts but a single leaf (36) that stands, in turn, for all its foliage. The leaf is an example of indicating a set by a single extract; the circle no doubt derives from a memory-image "selection" of roundness as the trunk's most essential attribute. The perspective of the horizontal cross section of the trunk, exactly at right angles to that of most other constituents of the picture, is consistent within the standard "inconsistencies" characteristic of memory images.

Also seeming to grow out of the tree is a giant eye (34) whose pupil is exactly on the horizon line, as if the scene were laid out in perspective according to that eye's position[15]—a situation that identifies it with the eye of the painter himself. Indeed, the extraordinary adventures and metamorphoses of the disembodied eye, as it traverses so many of Miró's pictures of the twenties, reinforce its identification with the artist's persona—a not unknown symbolism,[16] and one which would certainly occur to a painter whose very name means "he saw." Autonomous eyes, eyes growing out of landscape elements, and supplemental eyes growing out of animals were familiar to Miró from Romanesque art (fig. 7) and from the paintings of Hieronymus Bosch.[17] Closer to Surrealism were the mysterious disembodied eyes to be found in the work of Redon[18] and — in the years just prior to *The Hunter* — of Max Ernst.[19] But while the giant eye in *The Hunter* may be read as growing out of the tree — and this has been its standard interpretation — it may also be read as situated at "infinity" on the distant horizon (this would explain why it is only partially visible through the carob tree); indeed, Miró himself does not necessarily identify the eye in this picture with the carob tree.[20]

The sky of *The Hunter* is dominated by a sun (also described by Miró as a solar egg) from which emerge tentacle-like rays.[21] The sun's affinities in form and color with the sex of the hunter (24) and with the reproductive organ of the giant sardine below (57) allude to its life-giving power, and also measure the pervasiveness with which Miró was adapting Surrealism's "sexual myth." Further confirmation of Miró's association of the sun with sexuality and procreation is suggested by the fact that its shape — especially its wavy distensions — is very similar to that of the sex of the "mother" in *The Family* (p. 29), executed shortly afterward. (This same type of *sol genitor* is visible through a window in *The Harlequin's Carnival*, fig. 10, a picture which Miró began just after *The Hunter*, where the sun is "rhymed" visually with a creature at the center that the artist identified in a subsequent poem on the work as "a woman's sex in the form of a spider.")[22]

Sunlight fills the entire sky (32) of *The Hunter* with a transparent yellow, as it does also the sea (31) — presumably through reflection. Like the seagulls on the right, the sun itself is seen largely in silhouette. There is a rainbow (7) in the sky, the pattern of which inverts the converging arabesques of the peasant's *barretina*, and just to the rainbow's left, a star (6), whose rays resemble those of the light in the giant eye on the horizon. Then near the margin of the picture, symmetrical in placement with the seagulls on the right, flies a bird that is also an airplane.

Attached to the plane's body (3) is a wheel that Miró identifies as a propeller (seen frontally). This shape, which reappears in many guises in Miró's pictures of the twenties,[23] is derived from the machine imagery of Picabia — especially his *Novia* (fig. 13)[24] — which Miró knew well; its rubegoldbergian function here is also very close to Miró's Picabiaesque drawing, *Automaton* (fig. 14), executed about the time *The Hunter* was completed. The

wheel may also represent an unconscious echo of that motif in paintings by Hieronymus Bosch,[25] such as *The Haywain* (fig. 15), a fantastical forerunner of *The Farm*.

Hanging from the body of the bird-airplane is a ladder that seems to make the plane almost accessible from the horizon. Miró recalls that the airplanes of those days — and this image was inspired by the plane that regularly flew over Montroig on the Toulouse-Rabat run — had rope ladders, which were let down on landing. Like the wheel, the ladder first enters Miró's art during his realist period as an implement of the farm. From this point on, however, it was to be endowed with diverse poetic and metaphysical properties. In *Dog Barking at the Moon* (fig. 16), the ladder leads into an empty sky, that is, as Miró puts it, "to infinity." Then in *Landscape with Rooster* (fig. 12) it is juxtaposed (as in *The Hunter*) with a wheel, which hangs over the horizon like a vision from Revelation. (The wheel's apocalyptic content is even more explicit in the extraordinary *Somersault*, fig. 11, executed shortly after *The Hunter*, where it is juxtaposed to a horse falling through the sky, an image comparable to one in the Apocalypse of Saint-Sever, fig. 17.)

The two remaining components of the airplane — which Miró has also referred to as a "mobile construction" — are straight lines which cross to form an X. At the extremities of the line that represents the fuselage are a "tail" — much in the form that Calder would later use — and the crossed flags of Catalonia and France. The latter refer, of course, to the two homes of the "international Catalan," indeed the two heritages that fuse in the work.[26]

In apposition to the plane's two flags, the Spanish national flag (39) flutters in the wind on the right of the picture; its mast soars from an inverted cone that Miró has identified as a fisherman's bark (37). A strong descending accent in the composition, the bark, whose shape both echoes and inverts those of the "landscape elements" and the rifle, counteracts the upward movement of the horizon line (which tilts curiously as if in response to the downward movement of the shoreline).

Miró's choice of yellow for the sea makes for a particular unity of surface in *The Hunter*. Whereas the horizon line normally divides a landscape into two distinct sections, the upper one tending to be read as farther back in space, the Mediterranean here becomes a mediating area, belonging to the earth but having the color of the sky. As the yellow is warmer and more saturated than the terra-cotta rose of the earth, the upper section of the picture tends not to recede but cling to the picture plane. Moreover, the loosely brushed surface of this picture, so different from the tightness and opacity of the preceding ones, both allows the work to breathe and implies an indeterminate atmospheric space in a picture that is otherwise entirely free of conventional illusionism, i.e., perspective devices and sculptural modeling.

The thinned-out, "frescolike"[27] colors of *The Hunter* are applied with an almost Matissean ease. Miró had grasped from Matisse that thickness of *matière* not only fails to enhance color, but actively detracts from it by involving the eye with the perception of the material substance of the paint and by almost automatically tending to shade that substance. In brushing the color out, Miró disembodied it, achieving a transparency and luminosity by means of the gesso priming that is refracted through the colored glaze. Although Miró was to make tightly painted pictures throughout his career, the relaxed, easygoing facture of *The Hunter* and the slight spatial indeterminacy it invokes were to become particularly identified with his work.

Just to the right of the perforated triangle that Miró has identified as the grapevine[28] is a black triangle with wavy attachments (58) that is the tail of a sardine, whose form dominates the bottom of the painting. The freedom with which the sardine is "displaced" from the sea—a classic example of Surrealist *dépaysement*—is made possible by Miró's adaptation of the "inconsistencies" of imaginative (or memory) images. Attached to the fish's spine (54), which connects its black tail to its yellow head, are its eggs (57), its bowel (56), and its bones (55). In all, it forms an elegant, deftly articulated construction that clearly prefigures such Calder images as *Lobster Trap and Fish Tail* (fig. 19). Miró's sardine has sometimes been wrongly taken for a rabbit,[29] probably because its ear (53) is rabbitlike and because it is superimposed on the landscape rather than the sea. Partly as a clue to its identity, Miró placed the first four letters of the word *sardina* (46) adjacent to the fish's head, but these have been widely misconstrued in the literature as a reference to the *sardana*, a Spanish folk dance.[30]

Traversing the sardine's head is a heavy, wavy line (51) that represents the water's surface, and thus constitutes an autonomous "ground line" not unrelated to those of the potato (44), grill (41), and pepper (43). (It is evocative too of those figures in ancient Egyptian painting—also an art involving stylized memory images—who seem to come equipped with their own ground lines.) The eye of the fish is thus below water-level while his whiskers and tongue protrude. He has surfaced to eat a fly (47), which defecates (48) in fright.

As in certain prehistoric, archaic, and medieval styles, the size of some individual constituents of Miró's images is a function of their importance rather than of position in perspective space. Hence the monumental size of the sardine. Miró loved to look at sardines; he speaks of a particular vision of them as a kind of epiphany, and describes the unloading of the catch, when "thousands and thousands of sardines would be shining forth and shimmering like slivers of silvered metal." These multiple points of sparkling light create an effect analogous to that of fireflies, sparks, and stars—all of which would later be generalized in Miró's iconography by what he terms *les étincelles* (literally, sparks), and would inspire such "all-over" flickering compositions as the "Constellations" (page 81) and *The Song of the Vowels* (page 97).

Miró's poetic, almost metaphysical interest in sardines reminds us that while most of the motifs in *The Hunter* are schematic stylizations and transpositions of real landscape elements, their prosaicness is sometimes transfigured by the universal, quasi-mythic implications inherent in Miró's schematic-symbolic style itself—as, for example, the sun, which is also an "egg" and which relates to his imaging of both the male and female genitals (see above). The most purely "metaphysical" of all the motifs in *The Hunter*—one which cannot, like most of the others, be rationally assimilated to the iconography—is the flame (26) that rises from the sea to the left of the title figure. Its presence, in the first instance, responds to the fact that Miró no doubt wanted, at that place in the composition, to repeat the flame and/or smoke motif (Miró at that time generalized the two) of the campfire (42), rifle barrel, and pipe. But this particular flame is of a different symbolic order. Miró speaks of it as representing the "element" of fire, which with the earth, air, and water "completes the alchemy of the picture." A not unrelated "metaphysical" flame is isolated against the sky in the view through the window of *The Harlequin's Carnival* (fig. 10). "At the time," Miró observes, "both Masson and I were very much engaged with images of flame." Indeed, the Masson painting which first drew the attention of Breton, to whom

Masson soon introduced Miró, was called *The Four Elements.*[31] Moreover, the process by which Miró's iconography was increasingly generalized during the late twenties—the iconographic references becoming less anecdotal and more ambiguous, hence syncopated—paralleled Surrealism's growing concern with metaphysics and alchemy, concerns that dominated the second Surrealist Manifesto.

In contrast to motifs such as the large flame, which satisfied simultaneously both compositional and iconographic needs, there are a few signs in *The Hunter*—all of them dotted lines[32]—that Miró inserted "purely for the sake of equilibrium." These include the large V shape below the rifle, the repetitions of the oval sardine bone, and the meandering line behind the torso of the hunter. The latter, says Miró, "might be construed as indicating the volume of the hunter's body, just as the dotted lines of the sardine allude to its volume, but the decision to introduce them was entirely based on compositional needs."

Although the motifs of *The Hunter* vary in size, the marked hierarchy that characterized Miró's compositions right up through *The Tilled Field* has here been modified in favor of more evenly accented units dispersed over the whole of the field. While the hunter and carob tree are relatively large, the former is a transparent linear figure, while the latter functions as a lighter accent than many of the smaller forms because of its cream color's recessiveness and lack of visual "weight." Although the sardine is the largest motif, traversing over half of the composition, it is actually experienced visually as a series of discrete forms distributed along the bottom of the picture.

It would be an exaggeration to speak of *horror vacui* in the configuration of *The Hunter,* but there is an unquestionable tendency toward alloverness in the accenting, toward filling the space of the field. Miró brought this type of distribution to its first full realization shortly afterward in *The Harlequin's Carnival* (fig. 10). Such anticipatory "allover" configurations then disappeared from Miró's art, to be resurrected in the late thirties in his "Constellations" (page 81). *The Hunter* is less advanced into alloverness than *The Harlequin's Carnival.* But it has a grace and fragility missing in the latter. Its airy tracery initiated a kind of drawing that would characterize the abstract, "automatic" side of Miró's art from 1924 to 1928, the paintings which are today considered his most daring and—in terms of later abstract painting—his most prophetic.

THE FAMILY. *Paris, early 1924. Black and red chalk on emery paper, 29½ x 41 inches. (C&N, p. 116)*

In autumn 1923 Miró returned to Paris from Montroig and once again installed himself on the Rue Blomet in Gargallo's old studio. From then through the following winter he was largely occupied by a series of oils which have come to be known as "gray grounds," because of their paucity of color. While *The Family* is actually a drawing, indeed, a very elaborate one in chalk and charcoal on pastel paper, it is not, as are most of Miró's drawings of the time, a study for a painting. Rather it is a fully elaborated picture that "despite this [its] difference of medium . . . possesses all the features of the gray grounds and may justly be regarded as one of the most important of them."[1] Like Miró's paintings of 1924–25, it was preceded by preparatory drawings; this fact, in combination with the many pentimenti clearly visible in the work, indicates that Miró was still implementing his imagery slowly, adjusting the forms painstakingly, in the manner he had described almost two years earlier in his letter to Tual (page 19). Miró has indicated that he originally planned to finish *The Family* as a pastel; hence his choice of a special paper.

The protagonists of *The Family*, Miró says, were conceived as a bourgeois rather than a peasant trio, consisting (from left to right) of a father, mother, and little boy. Although they are presented frontally, almost hieratically—as in old-fashioned family photographs—the situation is, in fact, a relaxed and casual one, as evidenced by the gesture of the father who, holding a newspaper (13) in his right hand, has taken off his shoes (16) and socks (17). A pair of dice next to him (15) implies, Miró observes drolly, that "no husband is perfect." On one side of the child is his soccer ball (27), and on the other his hobbyhorse (39), the latter a more prosaic version of the central motif in the contemporaneous *Toys* (fig. 21). The giant Redonesque eye peering through the window suggests the inescapable presence of the artist himself. (The family, says Miró, "is glimpsed in the intimacy of their home.") The eye is frontal, as are the figures. Unexpected, and rather amusing, given the transient character of the motif, are the frontality and verticality of the wasp (37), situated like a heraldic image between the boy's head, the window, and a piece of furniture (38); the same conical form that had stood for "landscape elements" in *The Hunter* is here transformed by a simple contextual shift—moving it indoors, where as furniture it may be said to form the "landscape" of the room.

The father's head (3) consists of a near-circle of black embellished by a moustache (4); his toupeelike hair (almost caricaturing him as a bourgeois) and his eyes (2) are attached to the upper and lateral extremities of a rectilinear armature in a manner that Miró would repeat again in *Head of a Peasant* (fig. 22) and *Head of a Catalan Peasant* (fig. 23), both executed the following year. The father's pipe (5), which gives off a wisp of smoke, emerges from near the intersection of the vertical and horizontal lines of the armature. Further down his vertical "backbone," which ends in a disk that may be read as his sex surrounded by hair (8), we see the father's ribs (6) and bowels (7); his triangular legs—which pentimenti suggest were originally conceived as checked trousers—terminate in what Miró has identified as slippers (12).

The figure of the mother has much in common with "Madame K.," whose "portrait" (fig. 18) Miró executed during the same period. Like Madame K., she wears a jeweled pin in the form of an arrow (20), and the amatory character of her heart is expressed by an extrusion of little flames,[2] a symbolic motif found also in Madame K. and the Catalan hunter. The hairs (19) extend from the mother's head somewhat like the sun's rays in *The Hunter*, suggesting a sunflower; her body is a stem from which the breasts (21) emerge like buds, and her sex (23) resembles a bulb planted in the earth whose radicles are her pubic hairs. The mother's legs are drawn in "stick-figure" manner with only her right foot visible (25), the left obscured by the soccer ball. Despite the vegetal nature of her body, she is firmly "planted" indoors, the square below her right foot indicating the ceramic tiles of the floor (26).

The association of sexuality with vegetation is, to be sure, a commonplace; remarkable here, however, are the wit and imagination with which Miró realizes the metaphor. Its counterpart is to be found in *The Trap* (fig. 24), executed around the same time, where the lower body of a male personage whose erect penis ejaculates his seed into the earth is transformed, as it proceeds upward, into a plant stem that terminates in a sunflower.

A single arabesque represents the arms (14, 29) of both husband and wife and loops over to continue as the arms of the son (30)—thus indicating schematically that the three are holding hands. The son is rather summarily conceived, his feet (35) forming a "stand" from which rises the narrow cylinder of his body (33) to which his sex (34)

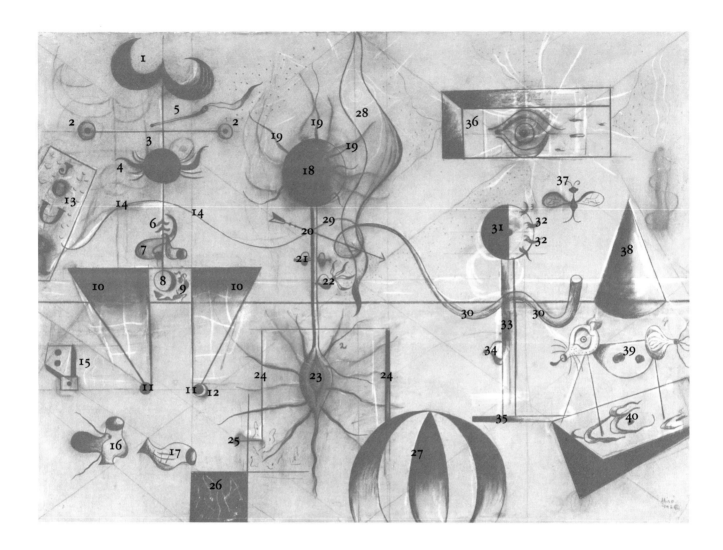

THE FAMILY

1. Father's hair
2. Father's eye
3. Father's head
4. Moustache
5. Pipe
6. Ribs
7. Bowels
8. Sex organ
9. Hairs
10. Leg
11. Foot
12. Slipper

13. Newspaper
14. Arm
15. Dice
16. Shoe
17. Sock
18. Mother's head
19. Mother's hair
20. Jeweled pin
21. Breasts
22. Heart
23. Mother's sex organ
24. Leg
25. Foot
26. Floor tile

27. Soccer ball
28. Flame
29. Mother's arm
30. Son's arm
31. Son's head
32. Son's hair
33. Son's body
34. Son's sex organ
35. Son's feet
36. Window
37. Wasp
38. Furniture
39. Hobbyhorse
40. Wood grain of hobbyhorse stand

is appended. The boy's circular head is divided vertically down the center into light and dark areas, echoing the contrasts in his soccer ball below. The fact that his hair is on the right suggests that his face is inclined toward his mother's. His hobbyhorse, posed on a stand whose wood grain is indicated (40), has a vegetable head and tail; the latter has been described by Miró both as a garlic and as an onion.

Close study of the surface of *The Family* reveals a series of faint vertical, horizontal, and diagonal lines. These indicate that despite the drawing's myriad curvilinear and biomorphic motifs and the apparently random spotting of its forms, it is actually held together by a quasi-Cubist grid. In fact, Miró has referred to this practice as "a hold-

over from my Cubist days." (Indeed, although no grid is manifest in *The Hunter*, Cubist structure had less disappeared than gone underground.)

The compositional field of *The Family* was originally subdivided by three equidistant vertical lines, three equidistant horizontal ones, and three diagonals in each direction, two of the latter connecting the four corners of the image. To this network Miró added a number of additional lines after inserting certain motifs. Thus, while the lower of the two dice sits exactly on one of the three horizontals of the grid, the "orthogonal" of the lower shaded face of the larger dice occasioned an additional diagonal that continues to the bottom of the picture; the heel of the shoe (16) is adjusted to just touch the intersection of two of the diagonals, while the top of the shoe is tangential to another. By the same token, the sock, while laid out along the new diagonal, is so adjusted that its tip just touches the intersection with the diagonal that joins the lower left and upper right of the composition.

Instances abound of Miró's placement of forms along the grid and its subdivisions (although in elaborating the composition he tended progressively to move the forms off these "architectural" accents). The sill of the window (hence the bottom of the giant eye) is set along one of the horizontal subdividers, and the orthogonal of its reveal is a segment of one of the diagonals; the child's left "hand," the mother's heart, the father's circular "pelvis," and the bottom of the newspaper are all located along the erased (but still visible) horizontal axis; the giant eye, which was originally centered on the vertical axis of the field, as erasures show, was finally centered on the vertical which subdivides its right side; the comparable vertical on the left provides a contour for the father's left trouserleg as well as the edge of the dark square of flooring; the short side of the surface of the hobbyhorse stand runs along a main diagonal.

For all these examples, however, there are many more instances in which Miró has aligned forms either with the less accented subdivisions of the grid or independently of it. For example, the pentimenti show that the vertical of the stick-figure father was originally placed on a subdivision of the grid one-eighth of the way from the left side of the field, where it terminated so that the central point of the father's hair just touched the main diagonal joining the upper left and lower right corners of the field. Subsequently, however, Miró moved the father's body somewhat to the right and tilted it slightly.

While later decisions thus tended to deemphasize the underlying grid, the reverse occasionally obtained. The large flame (28), for example, now to the right of the mother, rose originally on her other side along an axis that was not an accent of the grid. Miró subsequently moved it directly onto the central axis of the composition and carried its tip up to touch the junction of the vertical bisector and the two diagonals that meet at the top-center of the field. Iconographically, this flame, which Miró has characterized as a flame of maternal love, contrasts with the prevailingly anecdotal and concretely understandable motifs of *The Family*; it belongs to the same metaphoric order as the "metaphysical" flame that rises from the sea in *The Hunter*.

THE BIRTH OF THE WORLD. *Montroig, summer*[1] *1925. Oil on canvas, 8 feet ½ inch x 6 feet 4¾ inches. (C&N, p. 116)*

Late in 1924 Miró developed a new manner of painting, which in the originality of its means and effects remained unrivaled until the work of Jackson Pollock more than two decades later. This spontaneously executed, manifestly post-Cubist type of picture dominated Miró's output in 1925 and continued to play an important role—alternating with images in a painstaking, precise style—until the end of the twenties. Indeed, the new manner and the "automatic" techniques by which it was effected have, with modifications, remained basic to Miró's arsenal ever since. *The Birth of the World*, executed in Montroig in the summer of 1925, is his masterpiece in this style.

The new method, which involved loose brushing, spilling and blotting thinned-out paint in tandem with cursive, automatic drawing, not surprisingly led Miró to a larger average format. But even among his new large canvases, *The Birth of the World* (slightly over eight by six feet) was exceptional in size—which intensified the effect of its unexpected style. An extraordinary challenge to the conception of easel painting that obtained at that time, *The Birth of the World* was to enjoy an underground reputation among a handful of the artists and critics who saw it in the studio in 1925–26. However, the response of most viewers—even of those interested in Miró's work—was negative, and until after World War II this was the prevailing attitude toward all of Miró's paintings in this style. René Gaffé, the pioneer Belgian collector who purchased *The Birth of the World* the year following its execution,[2] spoke of the reactions of his collector and critic acquaintances: "It goes without saying that they took Miró for a madman, a hoaxer, or both. But they took me for an even greater fool for having bought the picture. The informed opinion of the day was that I had been taken."[3]

Gaffé developed an extremely protective stance toward *The Birth of the World*, never allowing it to leave his home until its first brief public exhibition in Brussels over thirty years after it was painted;[4] it would not be shown again until The Museum of Modern Art's "Dada, Surrealism, and Their Heritage" in 1968 and has never been publicly exhibited in Paris.

The "underground" reputation of *The Birth of the World* was certainly among the considerations that led André Breton in the middle-fifties to liken it to Picasso's

Demoiselles d'Avignon, itself not publicly exhibited or reproduced until many years after its execution; but when Breton called *The Birth of the World* "the *Demoiselles d'Avignon* of the '*informel*',"[5] he had primarily in mind the picture's radical character, large size, and, above all, the fact that it had anticipated the type of post–World War II painting known as *l'informel* in France (the counterpart of Abstract Expressionism in America). And earlier, in 1928, when Breton had written that it was "by such pure psychic automatism that Miró may pass for the most Surrealist of us all,"[6] he was thinking of Miró's improvisational, loosely brushed paintings of 1925–28 as a group, "but above all," he has pointed out, "of *The Birth of the World*."[7]

To be sure, the methodological automatism of *The Birth of the World* and Miró's other paintings in that manner was neither "pure" nor even as rapid or unedited as certain of Masson's works of the time. Nevertheless, its character is inconceivable without Miró's contact with Surrealist ideas, notably the definition of Surrealism as given in Breton's first Surrealist Manifesto of 1924:

SURREALISM, *noun, masculine. Pure psychic automatism by which one intends to express verbally, in writing or by other method, the real functioning of the mind. Dictation by thought, in the absence of any control exercised by reason, and beyond any esthetic or moral preoccupation.*[8]

Miró was impressed by the idea of automatism (and by the use Masson was already making of it in his drawings)[9] both as a mechanism for creating images which could be drawn from the artist's deepest instincts, impulses, and fantasies and as an antidote to the "rationality" of Cubist realism, against which Miró was then strongly reacting ("I shall break their guitar," he said of the Cubists).[10] Surrealist ideas had already influenced the paintings Miró had completed in 1924 insofar as the antirational character of the motifs depended on "free association"; this aspect of Freudian theory and the description of dream images constituted the dual underpinning of Surrealism, accounting for the two polar styles of its art.[11] But while free association led Miró to "irrational" juxtapositions of motifs in such pictures as *The Hunter* and *The Family*, the motifs there were sometimes much pondered, and aspects of their execution slow and painstaking.

Automatic drawing, on the other hand, allowed Miró to free-associate, in effect, on the canvas—to discover his motifs in the act of painting them. The difference may be measured by the fact that *The Hunter* was worked on over a period of at least eight months, while *The Birth of the World* was completed, Miró recalls, in two or three days. Surrealist ideas here suggested the *methodology* rather than the content of the picture—a methodology, however, for getting at a certain kind of content. Its application in the form of draftsmanly or painterly automatism led, as in *The Birth of the World*, to pictures of a very new appearance and character.

As observed above, this automatism was—Breton's formulation notwithstanding—far from "pure." Unrelentingly mediumistic, unconscious activity would be, in any case, inimical to picture-making. Automatism was used primarily to get the picture started and to provide its essential motifs. After that, the ordering of the canvas became a conscious proposition. The same obviously holds true for Surrealist texts. Indeed, it is clear that in Breton and Soupault's *Les Champs magnétiques* ("The Magnetic Fields") of 1919, later identified by Breton as "incontestably the first Surrealist work . . . since it was the fruit of the first systematic applications of automatic writing,"[12] the raw material of free association was subjected to no small amount of editing to arrange the flow of images in normal grammar and syntax. Later, Miró was to describe his somewhat analogous procedure:

. . . rather than setting out to paint something, I begin painting and as I paint, the picture begins to assert itself, or suggest itself under my brush. The form becomes a sign for a woman or a bird as I work . . . The first stage is free, unconscious . . . [But] the second stage is carefully calculated.[13]

Let us see how these procedures operated in *The Birth of the World*.

Miró began by covering the canvas with glue sizing that was purposely laid on irregularly, in varying densities. This was done so that the paint would take to the canvas unevenly, here consisting of a film atop the sizing, there impregnating or staining it. As a result the reflected light tended to vary slightly from point to point on the surface, thus enhancing the illusion of what Miró has called "an unlimited atmospheric space." The elimination of perspective devices goes so far as to include the horizon line—one of the first instances of this omission in Miró's art. This prevents the viewer from identifying the space as an extension of his own world and suspends the motifs in a kind of nongravitational universe.

After sizing the canvas, Miró rapidly laid down successive veils of transparent bister and black glazes. These were both poured and applied with the brush and, in some black areas, spread with a rag while still wet. Then a layer of ocher glaze was poured from the top, forming rivulets of greater density—hence opacity—here and there. Miró also dipped his brush in ocher and flicked it over the surface to create the "sprays" visible in particular in the lower part of the canvas. "One large patch of black in the upper left seemed to need to become bigger," Miró recounts. "I enlarged it and went over it with opaque black paint. It became a triangle, to which I added a tail. It might be a bird." The need for an accent of red to the right led Miró to make the carefully painted red disk with yellow streamer, which he later identified as a shooting star. These motifs and the nature of the ground, in turn, called forth the descending lines of blue on the upper right. The "personage" with a white head, whose right foot almost touches a spiderlike little black star, was the last motif to be introduced.

Miró has spoken of this picture "as a sort of genesis," and although the title, *The Birth of the World*, was invented by either Breton or Paul Eluard, as the artist recalls, it was very much in what Miró considered the spirit of the picture. As a genesis, it is the first of a long series of visionary Surrealist works which deal metaphorically with the act of artistic creation through an image of the creation of a universe. This iconography was extended by Masson, Ernst, and Tanguy in the late twenties and the thirties, and brought to a brilliant conclusion in Matta's *The Earth Is a Man* (fig. 25) of 1942 and *Le Vertige d'Eros* (fig. 26) of 1944. In the Mattas as in the Miró, the configurations lend themselves to being interpreted as both macrocosmic and microcosmic visions—the universe in terms of the poet's telescope or microscope. Or they may be seen as an image of the infinity of the recesses of the mind—the Surrealist "inscape"—embodied in a primordial galactic vision. *The Birth of the World* might also be thought of as a giant litmus paper stained with gray matter from which microbiological beings begin to emerge, a magnification of effects explored by Klee.[14]

The marriage of method and metaphor in *The Birth of the World* is total, for the imagery recapitulates poetically the process of its own creation. Miró the painter begins with an empty canvas—the "void." This is followed by a "chaos" of stains and spots. As he looks at these they suggest other forms to him; or he sees that they need to "grow" into another shape or color. The act of making the picture is thus literally the implementation of *miro-monde*, with the painter in the place of God as the "intelligence" behind the new universe.

The Birth of the World shocked Miró's colleagues not only for the sparseness of its configuration, but for the manifest role of accidental effects. Accidentality (what the Surrealists called *le hasard objectif*) merges here with automatism. But it is not the same thing. However "unconscious" the artist may be as he doodles, scribbles rapidly, or spreads liquid paint with rags, the impulse always comes from within the man. That his hand zigs here rather than zags there may feel totally undirected to him, and certainly, in comparison with traditional painting methods, it is. Nevertheless, on some level of the artist's functioning—however instantaneously it happened—a decision was made to do one thing and not another. Psychologically speaking, nothing the human being does is totally unmotivated, accidental. This does not apply, however, to the patterns made by liquid paint when it spills on a vertical surface, which are to some extent functions of the properties of the pigment and canvas and of the "laws" of gravity.

The value of such accidentality for Miró—as for Masson and other Surrealists—was that of a stimulus to pictorial ideas. (The starting point, for example, of one Miró painting was an interesting stain caused by blackberry jam that had fallen on the canvas. Miró developed the picture around it.) "These accidents are also a challenge," Miró has said. "The painter has to be like a seer; he has to make some sense out of them." Leonardo had written, as the Surrealists were well aware, of the value of stains and cracks in old walls and striations in marble as starting points for images. In the finished work, however, Leonardo's spectator was not to be aware of the image's sources. This precisely is what separates the modern picture from the Old Master one. Miró *wants* the accidents to be manifest—as he does his responses to them. The creative procedure, and thus to some extent the finished picture, is characterized by a world of forces in which everything is not entirely predictable a priori—an image of experience truer to the nature of twentieth-century life than are those of the closed universe of the Old Masters.

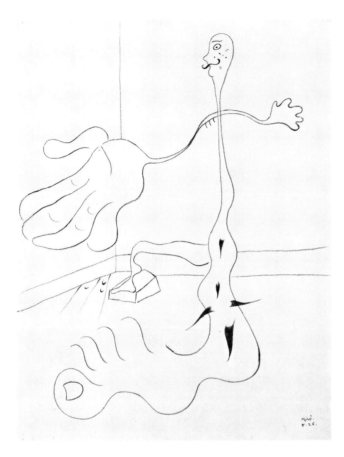

THE STATUE. *May 1926. Conté crayon on buff paper, 24½ x 18¾ inches. (C&N, p. 118)*

This drawing is a variation on a painting of the same title (fig. 28) that Miró had executed a year earlier. Both images portray a personage with a small head, a body with thornlike hairs—which may have inspired Giacometti's later *Disagreeable Object* (fig. 30)—and a very large foot, of which the big toenail is the salient shape. In both cases the figure is situated in a room indicated by the orthogonals of its walls and floor.

The figure in the Museum's drawing is more conventional than his predecessor. The silhouette of the head is here broken to indicate the nose and chin, and an eye, eyebrow, and moustache have been added; also, a right leg (as well as arms and hands) has been joined to what was earlier a single-footed creature.

The massive right hand and left leg are examples of a type of distortion rooted in what may be called the "internal image" of the self:[1] the way a part of the body *feels* as opposed to the way it looks. Such exaggeration would soon become central in Picasso's imagery, and it was, to be sure, in precisely the same year that Miró painted *The Statue* that Picasso's figures began to be radically distorted, although in a comparatively convulsive, expressionistic manner (as exemplified by his revolutionary *Three Dancers*, fig. 29).

FIGURE (*cadavre exquis:* sections from top to bottom by Tanguy, Miró, Max Morise, and Man Ray). *1926 or 1927. Ink, pencil, color crayon, 14¼ x 9 inches. (C&N, p. 118)*

The mystique of chance, of accidentality, deeply fascinated the Surrealists, and among the ways they explored it, beginning around 1924, was through a kind of collective collage of words and—soon afterward—images which they called *cadavre exquis* (exquisite corpse). The verbal form was based on an old parlor game: there were usually four or five participants, each of whom would write a fragment of a sentence (noun, adjectives, verb and direct object) on a sheet of paper, folding his contribution under so that it could not be seen by the next player, to whom he passed it on for additions. The technique got its name from results obtained in one of the earliest playings during the winter of 1924–25: "Le cadavre exquis boira le vin nouveau" (The exquisite corpse will drink the young wine).

These often surprisingly poetic fragments were felt to reveal mediumistically some unconscious sentiment of the group as a whole, resulting from a process that Max Ernst called "mental contagion." At the same time, they represented a transposition of Lautréamont's classic verbal collage ("beautiful as the chance encounter of a sewing machine and an umbrella on a dissecting table") to a collective level—in effect fulfilling his injunction, frequently cited in Surrealist texts, that poetry be "made by all and not by one."

It was natural that the Surrealists should seek through images as well as words such seemingly oracular poetic truths as the *cadavres exquis* might produce. The game was adapted to the possibilities of drawing, and even collage, by substituting the human body for the syntax of a sentence and assigning a section thereof to each player, beginning with the head and working downward. Despite this theoretical scaffolding, the Surrealist practice of displacement through metaphor often led to images hardly decipherable in anthropomorphic terms.

This *cadavre exquis* in the Museum Collection, begun by Tanguy and continued by Miró, Max Morise, and Man Ray in that order, is more easily readable as a humanoid form than most (for comparison, see fig. 31). Tanguy first drew a head with a naturalistic mouth, and eyes—extended to the sides on a kind of ribbon—as well as a number of fantastical extrusions, one an earlike form presented as a kind of vaginal leaf. Folding his drawing under so as to show Miró only the very bottom of the neck, he passed it on.

Miró's upper torso sports two breasts, one in profile and the other frontal. The nipple of the former has been pierced by an arrow around which Miró wrote its color indications: red, yellow, and blue. Given the seemingly cruel character of this motif, it is somewhat surprising to see, just below in parentheses, Miró's editorial exclamation, "How beautiful." But it may be that Miró considered the arrow—at least consciously—to be "costume jewelry," as he has so described those that similarly pierce the throats of the wife in *The Family* (p. 29) and the protagonist in *Portrait of Madame K.* (fig. 18).

The frontal breast is represented by Miró through concentric ovals somewhat in the manner of a contour map (it also resembles Père Ubu's paunch, or *gidouille*, as shown in Alfred Jarry's drawings)[1] and is surrounded by summary indications of shading. From the back of the figure projects a sharklike fish swimming between areas marked "Mediterranean" and "Atlantic," and above the fish soars a typically Miróesque bird-airplane. Between these two motifs Miró has interpolated the phrase: "besides, I don't give a damn."

After indicating the navel of the figure by a small black circle surrounded by radiants, Miró folded under his contribution and passed the paper to Morise. The latter drew a rather conventional lower female torso, added an arrow to the navel, and filled the left of his section with a series of overlapping numbers in perspective, probably inspired by related passages in Tanguy's work of 1926. Finally, Man Ray completed the figure with feet that seem to be snowshoes metamorphosing into squash rackets—which are accompanied by a group of what appear to be tennis balls.

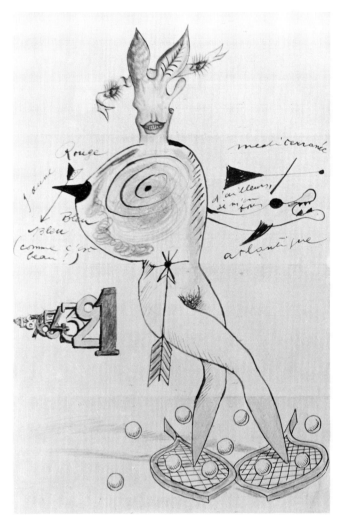

PERSON THROWING A STONE AT A BIRD. *Montroig, summer 1926. Oil on canvas, 29 x 36¼ inches. (C&N, p. 118)*

In 1926–27 Miró executed a number of landscape-type images that reflected a greater interest in anecdote than had been characteristic of the paintings of 1925. The motifs of *Person Throwing a Stone at a Bird*, particularly the bird itself, are relatively illustrative, and the horizon line immediately reestablishes a space more terrestrial than the apocalyptic reaches of *The Birth of the World*. The background of *Person Throwing a Stone at a Bird* is a beautiful triad composed of a yellow earth and a green sky separated by a black sea. The irregular shoreline, its pinnacles accented by grace notes of lavender and red, descants the almost straight horizon line, which is, however, as in *The Hunter*, slightly tilted.

The figure throwing the stone is an amoeboid biomorph with a Cyclopean eye and giant foot, seemingly derived — although not as directly as the drawing discussed above (p. 34) — from an earlier picture, *The Statue* (fig. 28). Its two arms are represented by a single straight line, next to which a lone dot was placed, Miró says, to indicate its center; this line is set crossbowlike against the curved dotted line that indicates the trajectory of the stone. A not unsimilar apposition is repeated in the straight body and curved wing of the bird, whose tail inverts the colors of earth and sky while its blue head and red crest provide the piquant color accents which resonate the large color fields of the composition.

As in the other landscapes of this series,[1] the execution is more closely controlled and the surfaces are more evenly applied than in pictures such as *The Birth of the World* — as if the relatively anecdotal character of the scene evoked a tighter facture. But while Miró's manner during these years oscillated between these modes, there was nothing programmatic about his method of applying the paint, and a variety of "handwritings" are often found in the same picture. Just as in *The Birth of the World* certain motifs were carefully drawn and evenly executed despite the prevailing painterliness of its handling, so in *Person Throwing a Stone at a Bird* Miró elected to make the sky brushy — and hence atmospheric — despite the picture's predominantly fastidious facture.

The biomorphic representation of the "personage" here shows Miró exploiting more emphatically than earlier what was by then the characteristic Surrealist form language, and one which by its very ambiguity enhances the possibilities of humor. Established by Arp, subsequently elaborated in personal ways by Miró and Masson, and later by Tanguy, Picasso, Dali, Matta, and others, this vocabulary of biomorphic shapes had arisen as an alternative to the prevailingly rectilinear structures of Cubism, and became established as the dominant morphology of the post-Cubist years.[2]

LANDSCAPE. *Montroig, summer 1927. Oil on canvas, 51⅛ x 76⅜ inches. (C&N, p. 119)*

This large and exceedingly spare picture (commonly known as *Landscape with Rabbit and Flower*) is the most dramatic of Miró's "landscapes" of the twenties. The drama derives not from its imagery, which is almost devoid of anecdote, but from its purely pictorial dynamics. The means used to achieve this pictorial tension were by now well established in Miró's work, but they are used here at their starkest, with little concession to charm. Of the three properties of color—hue, value, and chroma—Miró uses the latter two to maintain a unity of surface that embraces the contrasts of color and holds his entire composition to the plane of the canvas. He divides *Landscape* into an "earth" and "sky" of a red and blue that are of almost equal value and equal chroma or saturation. The pictorial drama established within these equivalences by the play of the blue against the red is reinforced by their contrasting factures—the flatness of the red against the painterliness of the blue. The latter's painterliness also suggests an atmospheric recessional space in the sky as distinct from the opacity of the earth—a contrast we see also in *Person Throwing a Stone at a Bird* (p. 36).

The "flower" in *Landscape*, which may relate to the "flowering rod" motif in Catalan Romanesque frescoes,[1] closely resembles the type of astral egg that Miró used to represent the sun in *The Hunter* (p. 23). Its associations with germination are reinforced by its appearance in the latter picture and elsewhere in Miró as a sign for genitalia.[2] (In *The Hunter*, both the protagonist's and the sardine's sexes are egg-shaped.) The egg-flower is also the only form in *Landscape* that is modeled, and therefore three-dimensional or "solid." As such, it serves as a foil that at once draws attention to the opaque flatness of the red and yellow and the liquidity, as it were, of the blue. Its "stem," a string anchoring the egg-flower to the earth like a balloon, serves as a vertical linear accent in opposition to the horizon line. Like the latter it is characterized by subtle changes of direction reinforced in the case of the vertical line by ever so slight changes in the thickness of the line, reflecting the changing pressures of the hand.

The almost colorless egg-shaped flower functions in a comparable relationship to the bright yellow color and scalloped silhouette of the whimsical animal in the lower left, which Miró has identified simply as the head of a rabbit.[3] Here, in the curious black "tongue" that breaks the silhouette and in the paired "ears," we encounter the only instance in this work where Miró has let his characteristic humor temper the seriousness and severity of the audacious conceit.

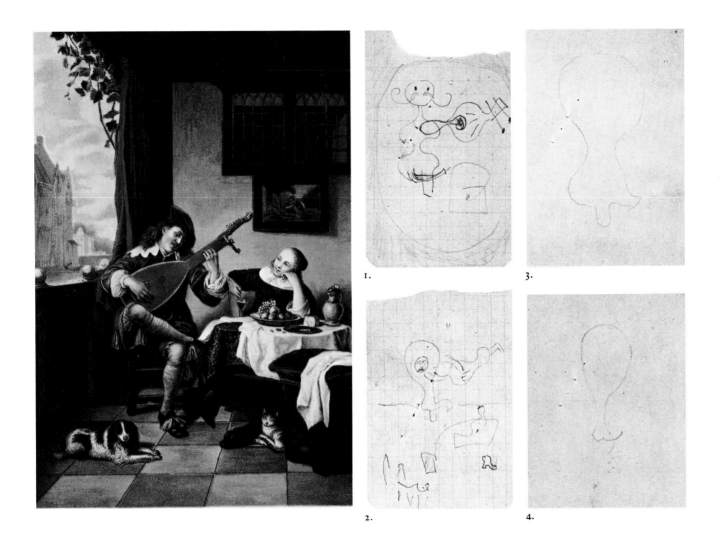

Colored postcard of Hendrick Maertensz Sorgh's The Lutanist, *1661; Rijksmuseum, Amsterdam. 5½ x 3⅝ inches. (C&N, p. 119)*

1. STUDY FOR DUTCH INTERIOR I. *Montroig, summer 1928. Pencil on graph paper, 3⅝ x 2¼ inches. (C&N, p. 119)*

2. STUDY FOR DUTCH INTERIOR I. *Montroig, summer 1928. Pencil on graph paper, 3¼ x 2¼ inches. (C&N, p. 119)*

3. STUDY FOR DUTCH INTERIOR I. *Montroig, summer 1928. Pencil, 6⅛ x 4⅝ inches. (C&N, p. 119)*

4. STUDY FOR DUTCH INTERIOR I. *Montroig, summer 1928. Pencil, 6⅛ x 4⅝ inches. (C&N, p. 119)*

8.

5.

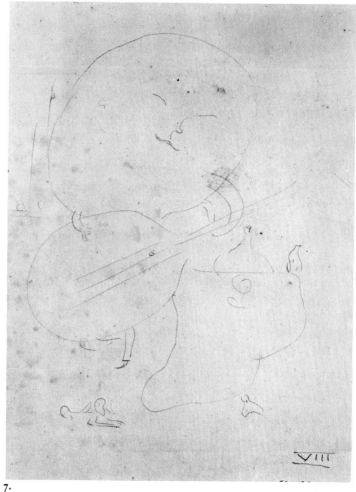

7.

6.

5. STUDY FOR DUTCH INTERIOR I. *Montroig, summer 1928. Pencil and white chalk, 6 x 4¾ inches. (C&N, p. 119)*

6. STUDY FOR DUTCH INTERIOR I. *Montroig, summer 1928. Pencil and pen and ink, 8⅜ x 6⅝ inches. (C&N, p. 119)*

7. STUDY FOR DUTCH INTERIOR I. *Montroig, summer 1928. Pencil, 10½ x 8 inches. (C&N, p. 119)*

8. CARTOON FOR DUTCH INTERIOR I. *Montroig, summer 1928. Charcoal and pencil, 24⅝ x 18⅝ inches. (C&N, p. 119)*

1. Vine
2. Clouds
3. Sky
4. Trees
5. Buildings
6. Bridge
7. Boat under bridge
8. Boat and oarsman
9. Window curtain
10. Baluster
11. Bird
12. Fish
13. Swan
14. Knife
15. Skin of apple
16. Apple
17. Frog
18. Insect
19. Dog
20. Ball for dog
21. Floor tile
22. Unwinding ball of yarn
23. Cat
24. Leg of stool
25. Cushion's drapery
26. Cushion
27. Footprint
28. Bat
29. Painting of Pyramus and Thisbe (see p. 119, note 4)
30. Leaded interior window
31. Ceiling plank
32. Bird with oval tail
33. Plume of hat
34. Hat
35. Lutanist's head
36. Moustache
37. Ear
38. Lutanist's hair
39. Lutanist's right arm and hand
40. Lutanist's left arm and hand
41. Lute
42. Sound hole of lute
43. Strings of lute
44. Small pegs of lute
45. Head of lute
46. Lutanist's right leg and foot
47. Garter on right leg
48. Left leg and foot
49. Leg of chair and small shadow
50. White tablecloth
51. Folds in tablecloth
52. Embroidered table-covering
53. Border of embroidered table-covering
54. Goblet
55. Book of music
56. Head of seated woman
57. Bust of seated woman
58. Left breast
59. Right breast
60. Heart
61. Pitcher
62. Loaf of bread
63. Left cuff
64. Bowl of fruit
65. Small plate

DUTCH INTERIOR I. *Montroig, summer 1928. Oil on canvas, 36⅛ x 28¾ inches. (C&N, p. 119)*

In the spring of 1928 Miró made a two-week trip to Holland, where he was greatly impressed by the seventeenth-century genre paintings. Their scrupulous realism and multiplication of detail, their anecdotal situations and intimate facture could not fail to strike a responsive chord in the painter of *The Farm* and *The Harlequin's Carnival*. Miró brought postcards of such works back to Montroig and during the summer used them as points of departure for his series of "Dutch Interiors." The Museum's picture—the first of three[1] titled *Dutch Interior*—is the most complex and ornamental of the group. Its intricate, "detailistic" character signaled a momentary return to a type of composition Miró had left behind with *The Harlequin's Carnival*. Indeed, *Dutch Interior I* represents the last appearance of this kind of configuration in Miró's art—save for a partial recurrence in the prolixity of the "Constellations" of 1939–40 (p. 81).

Dutch Interior I is a metamorphosis of H. M. Sorgh's *The Lutanist* (p. 40) of 1661.[2] Many of Sorgh's motifs—the lute itself (41), for example—are simply schematized by translation into Miró's now overwhelmingly biomorphic form language. Others are altered almost beyond recognition through enlargement (the head of the lutanist, 35) or diminution (the head and bust of the listening woman, 56 and 57). Through a process of aesthetic generalization Miró at once flattens, melds, and elides Sorgh's forms into continuous patterns that he invests with a sinuous rhythm absent from the original. This is most clearly illustrated by the leitmotif around which the composition's secondary forms are orchestrated: the extended white shape, traversed only by the orange of the lute, that runs diagonally through the picture. This form might be mistaken for the figure of the lutanist.[3] Indeed, the near oval section at the top does represent his head and collar: his long wavy hair (38) curling past his ear (37) emerges from this form; his displaced moustache (36) is situated on it; and his facial features are distributed in the red circle it surrounds.

But the remainder of the white form has nothing to do with the serenader. Miró determined its contours by generalizing the areas of high light value in the Sorgh painting, beginning with the head, collar, and right cuff of the lutanist, passing into the tablecloth, continuing with the face, upper bodice, and cuffs of the lady, and terminating in the folds of light cloth in the lower right. Through such condensations and metamorphoses Miró was able throughout to improvise an autonomous suite of abstract shapes that fit together like parts of a jigsaw puzzle. Suppression of all sculptural modeling—even such modest accents of relief as were to be found in *The Harlequin's Carnival*—locates the whole image directly in the picture plane, where the decorative colors, freed of the baggage of shading, shine forth in all their purity and saturation.

Miró translated the background and setting of Sorgh's *Lutanist* somewhat more literally than the figures. In the upper left of the *Dutch Interior* we can clearly make out the transposition of Sorgh's canal vista with its buildings (5), bridge (6), trees (4), clouds (2), and sky (3). As in the Sorgh, one boat passes under the arch of the bridge (7), while another (8) floats in the foreground; Sorgh's vine is clearly represented (1), as is his window curtain, whose folds Miró renders as brown arabesques (9); the closer of his two balusters is fully depicted (10), while the second (10) is shown without its finial. Miró has enriched Sorgh's scene by adding a fish (12), swan (13), and bird (11).

In the upper right of *Dutch Interior* we see the transposition of Sorgh's interior window (30), Miró's black triangular forms deriving from its tracery; on the wall below is a painting (29) that repeats the stabbing apparently shown in the Sorgh.[4] Other aspects of the setting that are equally legible include the squares of floor tiling (21) and the stool in the lower right (24), whose cushion (26) and drapery (25) are, however, rendered more abstractly.

Having undergone a more radical metamorphosis, the figure of the lutanist himself is more difficult to decipher. His velvet cap (34), to which Miró has added a colored feather, has become a minuscule shape perched atop the immense white oval of his head. In a whimsical insertion, the feather is about to be bitten off by the preposterous bird whose white oval tail (32) echoes in miniature the shape of the lutanist's head. Behind the bird, the indications of the ceiling planks (31), which Miró has transposed from vertical to horizontal accents, are not difficult to identify; on the other hand, one is quite likely to miss the diminutive crossed legs (46, 48) of the lutanist with his beribboned shoes and garter (47). Even more chimerical is the knobbed foot of the chair (49) on which he sits, which casts a tiny black shadow.

The earliest sketches for *Dutch Interior* are on the pages of a very small pad of the type that Miró carries in his pocket. The first shows the lutanist—endowed with antennaelike mustachios—reduced to an uncomplicated biomorphic form that nevertheless indicates his crossed legs. Sorgh's table is very summarily indicated, and the lute is curiously indicated twice, its more elaborate rendering set some distance to the serenader's left. In the second sketch, the lute remains at that distance, but is visibly attached to the player's arms. Here, for the first time, the lutanist's face is a circle inscribed within his free-form silhouette—essentially the formulation that appears in the final picture. This second sketch also establishes the contours of the listening woman in relation to the table and contains a contour line of drapery that leads to a shaded near-rectangle that would later emerge as one of the dark squares of flooring. The image also contains the first indications of a cat (in the lower right) and of what may be taken to be a dog and a rooster (in the lower left corner).

At this point Miró explored just the outer contours of the lutanist's body in two quick sketches that express the crossed-leg motif in different ways. These, in combination with the second sketch, were then extrapolated into the more fully developed fifth drawing in the series, in which the lute has a complicated configuration echoed in the contouring of the sexual organs with which the player has suddenly been endowed. This poetic association of the protagonist's serenade and his sexual ardor is found only in the fifth drawing; it then disappears from the evolution of *Dutch Interior*. However, Miró liked the drawing sufficiently to use it as the basis of a large collage (fig. 33) executed in the summer of 1929.

The antepenultimate sketch for *Dutch Interior* shows Miró still exploring different forms for the silhouette of the lutanist's body, although the latter's head continues to be conceived as an inscribed circle. The drawing is notable for the first indication of what appears near the right edge of the painting as an isolated black footprint. Though evidently linked to the lutanist in the sketch, it has in the painting the inexplicable mystery of one of de Chirico's disembodied shadows. When asked about the black footprint, Miró says only "someone was there." That "someone" would seem much in the nature of the presence whose eye peered over the landscape in *The Hunter* and through the window in *The Family*—that is to say, the alter ego of the artist, who has left behind the trace of his passage. (The trace of Miró's passage over the picture in a literal sense would later be marked in certain works by his handprint.)[5]

44

The penultimate preparatory sketch, though very casual in execution, establishes the shapes of the lutanist, his instrument, the listener, the table, drapery, dog, and cat in roughly their final form. But the leap between this and the definitive charcoal drawing is immense. A large number of secondary motifs metamorphosed from the Sorgh painting, and all those invented out of whole cloth by Miró as compositional "filler" make their first appearance only in this final study. Miró's own motifs include a frog (17, a marvelously intricate piece of patterning) which is about to gobble an insect (18), a laughing bat (28), and the bird (32) nibbling the lutanist's *panache* (33). These motifs, "invading" Sorgh's scene, intensify its conversion from commonplace reality to fantasy. Executed for transfer purposes on a grid, the large and exquisite final drawing served as the actual cartoon of the painting, and but for the differences in medium and size the two images are identical in almost every respect. The modeling in the drawing is of a clarity that permits us to confirm the reading of several motifs less identifiable in the painting itself, among them the trees and clouds seen through the window, as well as the latter's curtain. The most notable difference is in the definition of the fruit bowl, which is more detailed in the drawing. In the painting, the shape of the bowl has been changed into an open arabesque, and the fruit is reduced to a single dot.

Except for the dog in the foreground (19), which has been given a bone to munch on, and the cat (23), endowed in turn with a ball of yarn (22), the remaining salient motifs of Sorgh's picture are rather difficult to read in their "miromorphosed" form. The most radical transformations of all involve the listening lady and the tabletop. As we have observed, Sorgh's gracious listener has become a diminutive personage with only a black spot for a head (56). A black circle near her ocher heart (60) represents her left breast (58), while the right one is traced by the silhouette of her figure (59). Everything in front of her has been miniaturized, but the motifs are nevertheless identifiable. The book of music (55), goblet (54), pitcher (61), and loaf of bread (62) are simply stylized; a blue spot indicating her left cuff (63) issues into a line swinging down to an arabesque that Miró has identified as representing successively the folds in the tablecloth (51) and the fruit plate, the latter reduced to a tiny black dot (64). The green extrusion just below (51) was suggested to Miró by the folds of the cloth, and the black spot to which it is connected (65) represents the smaller plate on Sorgh's

table. In contrast to such miniaturizing, Sorgh's fruit—summarized by a single apple (and a knife that Miró has added to the props)—is much enlarged and situated on the floor toward the lower left.

The parallel black arabesques (53) within the white area below the table setting derive from the border pattern of the embroidered table-covering in the Dutch picture, and the area of the table-covering situated in the Sorgh between the book of music and the folds of the tablecloth is the source of the decorative triangular patch (52) just above the border pattern in the Miró. Here, in one of his most inspired passages, Miró sprinkled tiny circles and ovals of primary colors on a black ground—a kind of microscopic foretaste of the patterning of *The Song of the Vowels* of 1966 (p. 97).

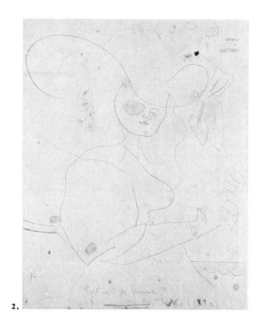

Photo of an engraving by T. R. Smith after George Engleheart's Portrait of Mrs. Mills. *10¼ x 8⅛ inches. (C&N, p. 120)*

1. STUDY FOR PORTRAIT OF MISTRESS MILLS IN 1750. *Paris, early 1929. Pencil on lined paper, 5¼ x 4¼ inches. (C&N, p. 120)*

2. STUDY FOR PORTRAIT OF MISTRESS MILLS IN 1750. *Paris, early 1929. Pencil, 8½ x 6⅝ inches. (C&N, p. 120)*

3. STUDY FOR PORTRAIT OF MISTRESS MILLS IN 1750. *Paris, early 1929. Pencil, 8⅛ x 6⅝ inches. (C&N, p. 120)*

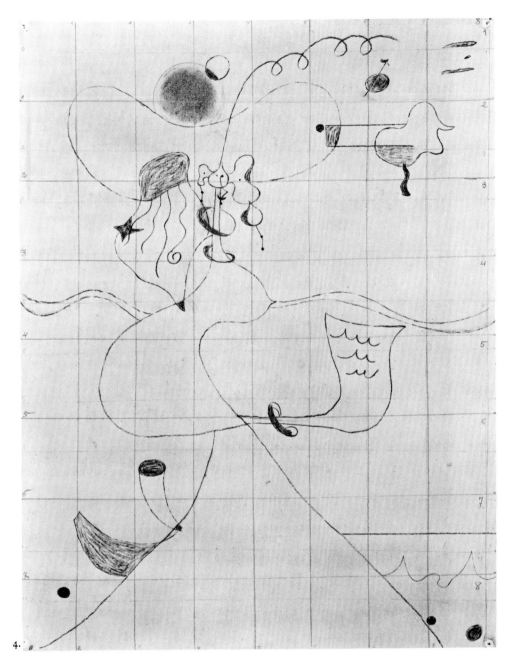

4. CARTOON FOR PORTRAIT OF MISTRESS MILLS IN 1750.
Paris, early 1929. Charcoal and pencil, 24¾ x 19 inches.
(C&N, p. 120)

PORTRAIT OF MISTRESS[1] MILLS IN 1750. *Paris, early 1929. Oil on canvas, 45½ x 35 inches. (C&N, p. 120)*

Portrait of Mistress Mills in 1750, after an engraving of a portrait of that lady (p. 46) by George Engleheart (1752–1829),[2] is the masterpiece of Miró's four "Imaginary Portraits," his most important series of 1929. Insofar as they were based on images of older paintings, the portraits reflect a continuation of practices established in the "Dutch Interiors." As a group, however, they are simpler, less anecdotal, and wander somewhat farther from the works that inspired them. The latter were less intricate than the Dutch genre paintings that had served as points of departure for the Interiors, and to which Miró had more closely adhered, in part, no doubt, out of affection. As the first of the portrait series, *Mistress Mills* is closest in style to the Dutch Interiors, being almost continuous with the third and last of them (fig. 32), a more loosely constructed and less painstakingly executed picture than the Museum's. At the same time, *Mistress Mills* is the most elaborate of the Imaginary Portraits, which became progressively austere.

The reproductions of the Old Masters used for the Portraits served virtually as substitutes for "automatic" doodling—a way of getting the picture started. As each portrait was developed through a series of metamorphic drawings, its expressive ambience became increasingly that of *miromonde*. Unlike Picasso in his extrapolations of the Old Masters begun a few years later,[3] Miró does not explore the psychology of the figures in his borrowed motifs or enter into their narrative situations. Rather he converts everything into his own terms, seizing more on the marginal aspects of the earlier pictures than on their total concepts. Thus Mistress Mills's face becomes smaller than her bright red left ear—and less visually engaging. And her ribbon, the broad ocher band that projects from her hat and terminates in a bow, becomes one of the most arresting and elusive shapes in the composition. Miró's eye was caught by the ornamental aspects of the Engleheart work; he cared so little for the original that he forgot the identity of its author.[4] (Picasso, in contrast, has always identified himself psychologically with Velázquez, Poussin, and other painters whose work he "re-creates.") Just as ornament is what attracted Miró in the Engleheart, so it is ornament that he adds to the conception, both on the illustrative and formal levels; he has, for example, put a spangled clasp in Mistress Mills's hair, and gifted her with a double necklace.

The metamorphoses of *Mistress Mills* out of Engleheart's *Mrs. Mills* may be observed in a series of four progressively more studied and more detailed drawings,[5] the last of which is a working cartoon for the Miró picture. The first is a very summary sketch in which Miró immediately indicates his intention to show more of the lady below the waist than had Engleheart. He also adds a bird in the background and inscribes the words *mon cheri* on the letter in Mrs. Mills's hand. The words were replaced in the next sketch by the wavy lines that obtain until the final picture (although in the penultimate drawing the English words "my dear"—subsequently crossed out—are visible below these lines).

The second sketch contains many more of Miró's definitive motifs. The interpenetrating pattern of black and white, which represents the stylization of Engleheart's light and shadow, is established in the lower right corner; a form suggesting a waistband-bow or bustle has been introduced behind the figure; her hair is spangled; the feather on her hat has been given its curlicue form; and the bird in the background is clearly described in what will remain its basic form as an arrow through a circle.

The reduction of Mistress Mills's head and neck to a narrow stem supporting a group of tiny biomorphs and the raising of the line of the couch to the level of the nipple of her breast are the most significant changes initiated in the third drawing. More carefully elaborated than its predecessor, this image also marks the introduction of details such as Mistress Mills's necklace and bracelet, and shows her hair and the spangles in it in what was to be their definitive form. Here for the first time the brim of the hat, whose arabesque in the earlier drawings had turned in space, has been flattened into a closed form, while the ribbons to the right and above it have been stylized much as we see them in the painting.

The fourth and final study represents essentially a clarification of the third—especially in the region around the hat—and a reworking of the contours to the precise configuration that Miró wanted in the painting. This charcoal drawing, like the last study for *Dutch Interior*, served as a cartoon for the picture, which is virtually identical so far as its contouring is concerned—even closer than is *Dutch Interior* to its cartoon.

In *Portrait of Mistress Mills in 1750* Miró achieved a compactness of design rarely matched in his later work, a compactness that results from equalizing the impact of figure and ground. In *Dutch Interior* Miró had squeezed both figure and ground into the picture plane, but only the figural elements were endowed with any significant definition as shapes; the dog, cat, frog, knife, and other details seen against the brown floor are fascinatingly contoured, but the brown area itself is just a foil, an unshaped *repoussoir*. In *Mistress Mills*, the reserve areas of vermilion on the left and red brown on the right against which the subject is set (and which may be identified with the *canapé* on which she sits) have an autonomous quality, a definition of shape comparable in interest to that of the contiguous green upper torso and brown skirt. As if to symbolize this equation of figure and ground, Miró included in the lower right corner of the canvas a kind of visual charade consisting of interpenetrating black and yellow abstract shapes—a stylization of the light and shadow areas in the same location in the Engleheart—either one of which may be read as figure or ground. This contouring of the surface in terms of more reciprocal figure/ground relationships was to prove very rare in Miró's works, which are generally composed of figures profiled against a less clearly defined atmospheric ground. Miró's ornamental line is more artless here than in *Dutch Interior* and his biomorphic forms simpler, perhaps reflecting the proximity of his friend Jean Arp, whose studio was in the Rue Tourlaque not far from the one in which Miró painted *Mistress Mills*.[6] Indeed, an unquestionable affinity has been pointed out between *Mistress Mills* and *Mme Torso with Wavy Hat* (fig. 38),[7] one of the finest of Arp's Dada reliefs, although the wavy form at the top of the Miró certainly derived more immediately from the Engleheart.

In *Dutch Interior* Miró had already established himself as a master colorist. In earlier pictures his prismatic colors were often muted, and when not, they were used primarily as isolated accents, while the blacks tended to work as local modeling more than as autonomous color. In *Mistress Mills*, Miró advanced to an even stronger reliance on pure color than in *Dutch Interior*, giving it a breadth and transparency[8] worthy of Matisse. Indeed, it was Matisse, Miró asserted, "who taught us that color alone . . . could carry [a picture's] structure through contrasts and subtle juxtapositions."[9] The large areas of prismatic hues dominate the ornamental drawing, and the blacks—now functioning as color areas rather than as shading or as contours—provide a foil for their brilliance.

COLLAGE. *Montroig, summer 1929. Pastel, ink, watercolor, crayon, and paper collage, 28⅝ x 42¾ inches. (C&N, p. 122)*

In the summer of 1929, not long after he had painted *Mistress Mills*, Miró executed this collage at his family home in Montroig. It evidences an even more marked tendency toward simplification and generalization of the forms than had the painting. We are here once again transported into a kind of microcosmic primal universe—different from but not unrelated to that of *The Birth of the World*—an ambience that is a metaphor for the recesses of the artist's consciousness. On the left, against a green ground, Miró has traced the contours of two amoeboid creatures; the larger rises from the lower left to greet its mate, whose single distinguishing feature is its circular black eye. The Arp-like simplicity of these biomorphic shapes is simultaneously echoed and descanted in the rough circular or rectangular contours of all the superimposed collage elements, with the exception of the bluish vertical that descends to the right of the central axis.[1] Only in the upper right, where the drawing is more intricate, do we find traces of the typical Miró of the mid-twenties.

The awkward, irregular edges of several elements in *Collage* bespeak an improvisational abandon comparable to that of Miró's freest paintings of 1925–26, and the purposely casual manner of the gluing was intended to leave a relief of crinkles and folds and to allow the edges of many of the forms to pull away from the ground.[2]

It is not impossible that Miró's concern for an unfinished look at that moment bore some relation to a crisis in Arp's work which began in 1929 and which led Arp to abandon temporarily his habitual notion of finish in a series of *papier-déchiré* collages.[3]

RELIEF CONSTRUCTION. *Montroig, summer 1930. Wood and metal, 35⅞ x 27⅝ inches. (C&N, p. 122)*

While many of Miró's 1928–29 collages contained slightly relieved elements (especially one version of *Spanish Dancer*, fig. 39, which incorporates a draftsman's triangle and a spike nail suspended from a string), it was only with his constructions of the summer of 1930 that the artist first confronted the possibilities of what may properly be called relief sculpture. The Museum's *Construction*, although the best known, is the least characteristic of this group, devoid as it is of the heterogeneous "found objects" which Miró used to compose the others. Indeed, its sobriety leans in the direction of Arp, who was shortly afterward to try (unsuccessfully) to lead Miró into the purist-oriented Abstraction-Création group. Even as compared to the morphology of Miró's oils of the previous year—for example, *La Fornarina* (fig. 36), the last and most schematic of the Imaginary Portraits, with which *Construction* has distinct affinities—the form language of this piece registers as relatively austere. To be sure, the precisionist aspect of its contouring probably owes something to the fact that it was, like Arp's reliefs, executed by a carpenter on the basis of a drawing by the artist.

Projecting forward from a rectangular ground composed of four unpainted vertical fir slats, a simple white torsolike shape is suspended by a hidden support; just above, a vertical metal spike rises toward a small disk of black; at the same height as the latter but farther left is a larger disk of red. Like the black one, it is attached directly to the surface of the field rather than being suspended from it. Miró has identified the spike and black disk as the neck and head of what the torso betrays as a feminine personage; the red disk is the sun. However abstract Miró's works of this period may seem—and one of the most daring is a large painting consisting of nothing more than simple disks of black, red, and yellow against a flat white ground (fig. 40)—it must be remembered that there is no such thing as a nonfigurative element in Miró's painting. However elliptical, however distant the allusion, every form in his paintings is associated metaphorically with something outside the work.

The interest in texture reflected in Miró's decision to leave unpainted the knotty and veined wood background of *Construction* is also evidenced by the metal staples distributed over the torso and the nails projecting somewhat menacingly from the red disk. By their somewhat random placement, these counteract the purist tendencies within the work and function as a counterpoise to any tendency toward charm; Miró says he intended them to carry connotations of discomfort and aggression. Picasso had four years earlier accented the contours of a collaged *Guitar* by hammering nails through the surface from behind (fig. 41); his avowedly aggressive intent[1] was in the line of a kind of tactile violence that we see in Giacometti's *Disagreeable Object* (fig. 30) and in numerous Miró drawings (fig. 42) as well as some paintings of the middle and late thirties in which the personage's clublike features and limbs develop thorny extrusions—as if teeth grew at random from them. Miró's intentions in *Construction* notwithstanding, the projecting nails and staples are ultimately absorbed in the prevailingly decorative effect of the work as a whole.

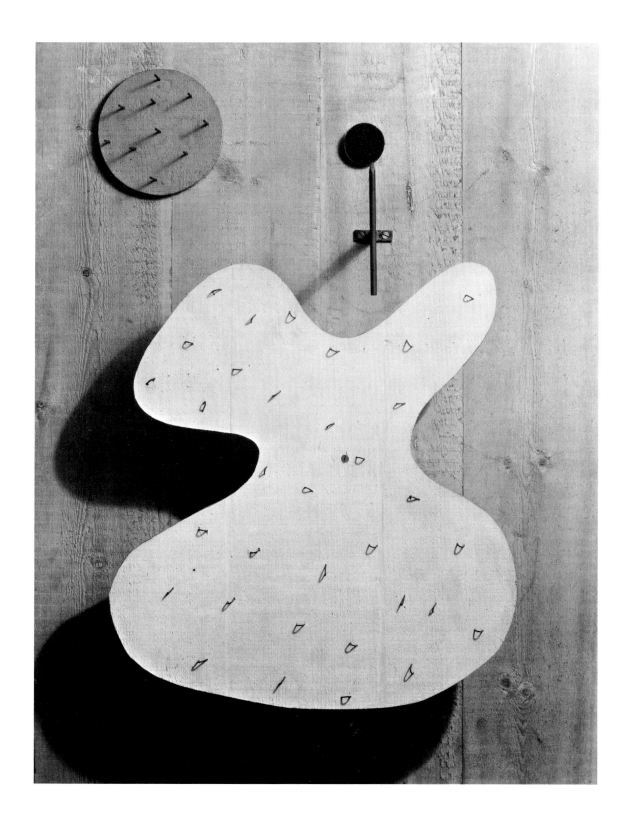

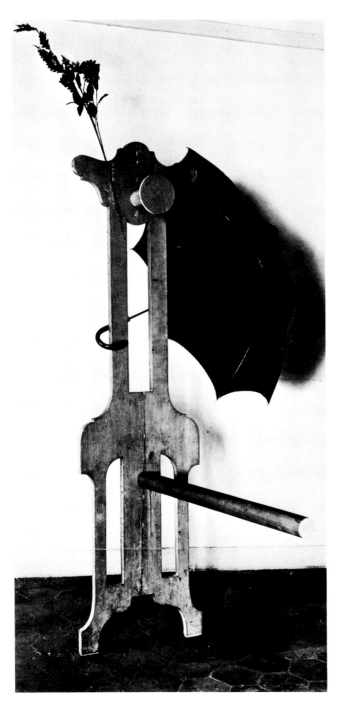

PERSONNAGE AU PARAPLUIE. *Montroig, summer 1931. Wood furniture frames, dowel, umbrella, and artificial flowers, c. 6 feet high. (C&N, p. 123)*

One gallery of the Salon des Surindépendants held in the autumn of 1931 was reserved for Surrealist art, and the selection of works was entrusted to André Breton. His most provocative inclusion — indeed, it proved a *cause célèbre* — was this object, which Miró had executed during his summer stay at Montroig. The provocation depended largely on the figure's immense phallus, which led some to suggest that it was meant as a "statue" of Alfred Jarry as *surmâle* (or "supermale").[1] This was not, however, Miró's intention, and in fact the object had grown out of his speculations on decor for a ballet he was contemplating in collaboration with his friend, the composer Georges Antheil. Miró had thought of concealing the dancers in large papier-mâché horn shapes from which an arm of one of the dancers would project holding an umbrella (fig. 43). (This particular ballet project was never realized, but some ideas from it will be incorporated in work scheduled for completion in 1974[2] in which Miró will collaborate with the choreographer Maurice Béjart.)

Personnage au parapluie suggested itself to Miró while he was examining furniture frames at a cabinetmaker's — a pastime that had its origin in the fact that his wife's relatives, on one side of the family, were cabinetmakers. Miró does not recall the type of furniture for which the frame, which he doubled symmetrically to form his personage, was intended. Once the frame was doubled, the top seemed to him to suggest a broad hat, or possibly an old-fashioned wig, so he added a disk just below to represent the face — and then the large dowel to serve as a phallus. Although an umbrella in Surrealist works automatically tends to bring to mind Lautréamont's famous image (see p. 34), it is here rather a symbol of the personage's conservative, "bourgeois" side. This is balanced by the sprig of paper flowers, projecting cavalierly from his bonnet, that endows him with quite literal *panache*.

OBJECT. *1931. Assemblage: painted wood, steel, string,*
bone, and a bead, 15¾ inches high, at base 8¼ x 4¾ inches.
(C&N, p. 123)

BATHER. *Montroig, October 1932. Oil on wood, 14¾ x 18⅛ inches. (C&N, p. 124)*

In 1931 Miró's work had moved tangentially from his established morphological universe into a more geometrically abstract world of forms in a series of oils on Ingres paper (fig. 44). In these, the areas of color—counterpointing rather than contained by the black lines—tend toward girder or bar forms, which give the series a distinctly architectural air. Although familiar motifs, such as birds, moons, and eyes, can be discerned, these pictures are unique in Miró's œuvre in the almost rectilinear character of their abstraction, and quite without either the decorative or expressive character of his arabesqued conceits.

A series of twelve small wood panels executed the following year witnessed Miró's return to his personal form language, but in a context in which the vestiges of rectilinear abstraction of 1931 remain as foils, intensifying the more properly Miróesque aspects of the composition. *Bather*,[1] an especially brilliant work in the series, exemplifies this polarity. Here, the baroque biomorphic female figure is set against a landscape of three horizontal bands absolutely rigid in their contouring and entirely purged of modeling or shading. While the sky is a naturalistic blue (and a setting sun of saturated red is suspended over the horizon), the sea is here an acidulous yellow, there white, and the beach is a green so dark as to be almost black. Given the mordant effects of the rusts, oranges, lemon yellow, red, and greens played off against one another, and the percussive contrasts of all of them in relation to the blue and deep green, Miró's coloring sustains the intensity established by his configuration as a whole.

If the rigidly banded background of the *Bather* is more geometrical and abstract than any landscape we have seen earlier, so the exaggerations of the biomorphic figure are in their turn more outrageously free. The bather appears to be seated at the edge of the shore line. Her head is so tiny that it seems an immense distance from her buttocks. The gargantuan orange tongue she sticks out toward the spectator traverses this immense distance, becoming as monumental in the foreground as the buttocks. The perspectival polarizations of size noted here are in keeping with the principle of contrast that animates the entire composition, and are reminiscent of similar unexpected juxtapositions of minuscule and monumental features in Picasso's Dinard bathers (the morphology of which was itself influenced by Miró). However, the contorted forms of Picasso's bathers reflect the tension and anxiety of a particularly problematic moment in the artist's life, while Miró's distortions of the female form are essentially impersonal. They express "nothing but their own intensity and continuous development . . . merely one variant possibility open to the morphology of the species. These bodies do not evade their humanity, but to the settled constitution that is ours they oppose *organic mobility*, a capacity for metamorphosis that has become atrophied in ourselves, and that we can now only conceive of in imagination."[2]

The torso of *Bather* is more difficult to decipher than are those of Miró's figures of the twenties because of its extreme distortions and displacements. A tear-shaped form does, however, suggest her breasts—one shown frontally, the other in profile. And slightly below and to the right is the aperture indicating her sex. As is not uncommon in Miró, the handling of these features seems to endow the torso with a "physiognomy" of its own, so that it may alternately be read as a face.[3]

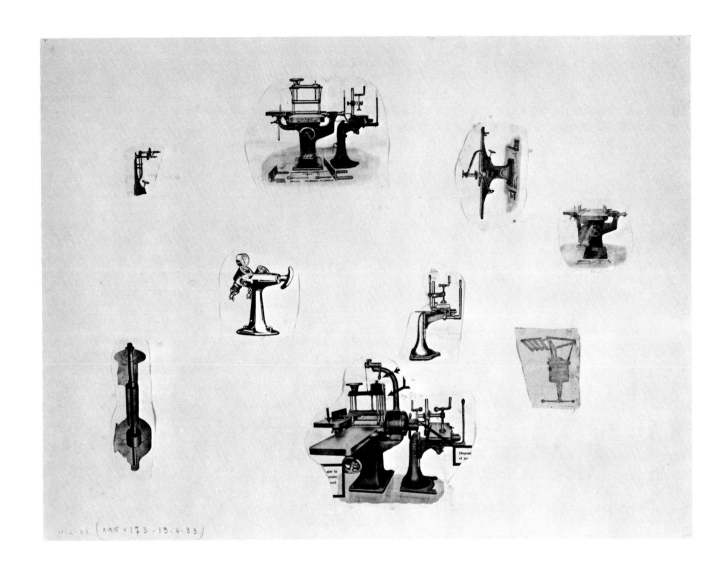

COLLAGE *(Study for* Painting, *1933). Barcelona, February 1933. Cut and pasted photomechanical reproductions and pencil, 18½ x 24⅞ inches. (C&N, p. 124)*

PAINTING. *Barcelona, June 1933. Oil on canvas, 68½ x 77¼ inches. (C&N, p. 124)*

Because of financial difficulties, Miró and his wife spent the spring months of 1933 with his parents in Barcelona. There, in the apartment in which he had been born, working in an attic room arranged as a studio, he executed a group of eighteen large paintings that in the consistency of their realization marked a new level of achievement for him.

These pictures also serve as a general index to the change that overtook his art in the thirties. The period 1924–29 had been characterized by an astonishing morphological variety and a constant invention of new compositional ideas. The thirties were more exploitative than explorative; there were, in comparison, fewer new ideas. But many possibilities first envisaged in the twenties were consummated only in the thirties. Intricate iconographic

programs gave way to less anecdotal conceptions realized in a more restricted vocabulary of signs; compositions became broader, simpler, and more monumental, their formats larger; as compared to the immensely variegated, minutely dosed palette of the later twenties, color became more luminous and was increasingly embodied in large areas of primary hues.

Like the other seventeen oils in this series, the Museum's *Painting* was based on a collage of images of machines and other utilitarian objects cut from catalogs and newspapers (p. 58). All eighteen collages were made before any of the paintings were undertaken, and were strung across the walls of Miró's little studio so that he could study them. The paintings were executed between March and June of 1933, often at intervals of just a few days. Each completed canvas had to be unstretched and rolled up to give the artist room to work on the next one.

The preparatory collage for *Painting* shows cutouts of machine tools[1] of differing size and complexity glued to a plain white ground. These forms played little or no role in the first phase of the painting, however, which involved the division of the canvas ground into soft-edged modulated rectangles of bottle green, smoky blue, dark rust, and brown. Such passages, which are luminous and atmospheric, functioned as foils for the biomorphic motifs inspired by the collage elements. The latter were painted over the rectangular grounds either as panels of flat opaque color (mostly black) silhouetted against the luminous atmosphere or as "transparent" figures, through whose firm outlines the ground is visible. While certain divisions of the background—the green rectangle at the top, for example—seem to have been suggested by the particular distribution of elements in the collage, the relation of the background panels and foreground motifs appears somewhat arbitrary.

As Miró translated his ideas from the collage onto the large canvas—working from the former, he recalls, as if *d'après nature*—the machine forms shed their details and their rigid contours to become simple biomorphs, wholly devoid of the meandering Art Nouveau contours and unraveling ornament of Miró's earlier drawing. Taken together, these shapes seem to suggest nothing so much as a serene pastorale of grazing and playing animals. Commentators have been almost universal in seeing horned quadrupeds and—at the upper left—a seated dog.[2] The forms in the lower center suggest an animal on its back playing with another—a motif also found in Klee, whose images

of fantastical animals (fig. 45) are often similarly suspended against vague atmospheric grounds.

It is, of course, futile (and undesirable) to assign specific meanings to the forms in *Painting*. Unlike those in the Dutch Interiors and Imaginary Portraits, which, despite their radical metamorphosis, never lost an elliptical link to their original identities, the configurations here have shed the appearances of machines but have not yet acquired those of animals. Neither, however, are they "pure" formal entities. More than in his works of the twenties Miró is here using biomorphism in the ambiguous spirit in which Arp had first used it almost two decades earlier,[3] choosing the form which connotes much but denotes nothing.

In *Painting* Miró was less dependent than heretofore on the improvisational aspects of "automatic" procedures. The picture is not implemented from *tabula rasa* as were such pictures as *The Birth of the World*. Nor is it an extended paraphrase of another work of art, as in the case of the Dutch Interiors and Imaginary Portraits. Despite the translation of machinery into Miróesque biomorphs, *Painting* (like the other pictures in this 1933 series) remains in terms of spatial disposition much closer to the collage on which it was based than was the case with the Interiors or Portraits, and to this extent it foreshadows Miró's brief return in the later thirties to working from the motif.

Something of the serenity, the relative detachment of *Painting* seems to depend upon this use of a model. Indeed, Miró appears to have purposely chosen machine forms for the preparatory collages—forms so alien in shape and spirit to his own organic world—in order to "set up a barrier . . . between his creative enthusiasm and the actual execution . . ."[4] The choice, however, also measures the distance Miró had traversed—in the sense that the machine forms were a conscious reference to the past, to the Dada paintings and cataloglike illustrations of machines by Picabia, whom Miró first met in Barcelona in 1917. (Indeed, we have seen the influence of these works in Miró's painting of the twenties).[5] But the mystery of the machine as such, and the idea of the machine as analogue of human functions, had no interest for Miró. We see none of the irony of Duchamp's machines, nor the wit of Picabia's, in Miró's picture. Nevertheless, *Painting* is imbued with a gentle and indulgent humor, expressed in part through the subsumption of the machine forms into what appears a more timeless, archetypal pastoral symbolism that reaches back as far as Miró's beloved Altamira caves.

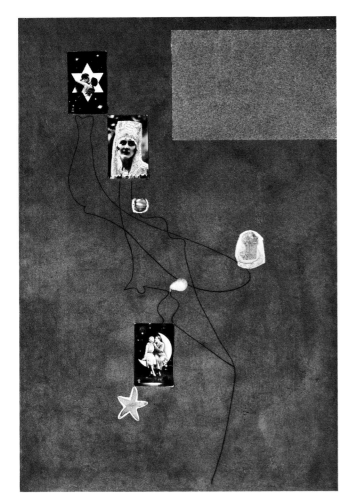

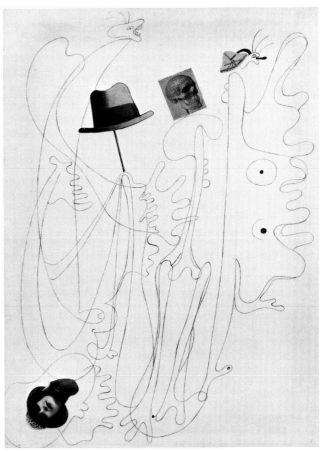

DRAWING-COLLAGE. *Montroig, August 1933. Collage and charcoal drawing on green paper with 3 postcards, sandpaper, and 4 engravings, 42½ x 28⅜ inches. (C&N, p. 125)*

DRAWING-COLLAGE. *Montroig, October 1933. Charcoal and collage of cut and pasted photographs and offset reproduction, 25⅛ x 18⅝ inches. (C&N, p. 125)*

During the summer of 1933 at Montroig, Miró allowed himself a respite from the rigorous concentration required by the eighteen large canvases and executed a series of playful collages, most of them containing outrageously sentimental postcards as well as irregularly shaped motifs cut from illustrated children's books and other sources. The Surreal formula of linking autonomous images by a linear armature differentiates these collages from Miró's more formal essays in this medium in 1929, and suggests Max Ernst's "Loplop Introduces . . ." collage series[1] (fig. 46) begun in the winter of 1929–30.

The sole echo of the structural interests of the earlier collages present in the *Drawing-Collage* of August 1933 is the iteration of the roughly 2:3 proportions of the rectangle of sandpaper (a texture that recalls the earlier collages) to the green-ground format of the work and then, in smaller scale, its reiteration in the proportions of the three postcards to the sandpaper rectangle. The rectilinear structure was then ornamented with four irregularly shaped cutouts tied together and to the postcards by a meandering line that suggests a female personage.

The eye-catching collage elements fit neatly into a whimsical iconography. The postcard of a girl in Spanish headdress provides the head of a film-struck maiden, young, pretty, and sentimental; not far down her neck is her Adam's apple, appropriately illustrated by a collaged apple.[2] Down past her breasts, the uterine contours of a collaged pear above a vulvalike form suggest the maiden's sexuality. As both a compositional and metaphoric counterpoise to the collaged postcard (above her head) of an embracing couple silhouetted against a star, there is, below her sex, another postcard of an amorous couple sitting on a moon with a pendant star (a cutout of a starfish). The ambience is that of the naïve romance of the earliest movies (the imagery is that of Méliès), to which these postcards, much loved by the Surrealists, relate directly. Indeed, the Surrealist poet Paul Eluard published a number of them at the very time that Miró executed this collage.[3]

Traversing the maiden's body is an elongated form on the right edge of which Miró has collaged the head and neck of an anatomical illustration, an *écorché*—literally, a "flayed man." While Miró no doubt felt he needed a light-colored shape here, he might have chosen any motif. But the inescapably phallic connotation of the skinned neck and head arching upward from out of a fleshy sheath at once extends the iconography through free association and provides a literal, tough-minded foil for the sentimentality of the rest of the imagery.

In the *Drawing-Collage* of October 1933, the last vestiges of the geometrical interests that had animated Miró's early *papiers collés* have disappeared in favor of an extraordinary richness in the drawing, the collaged elements serving as little more than grace notes to the linear melody. The combination of drawing and collage is more cohesive here than in the collage discussed just above; the eye is not seduced, as it is there, into focusing on the anecdotal elements, and the drawing has a celerity and freedom that show Miró's automatism at its best. The line seems to spin out its elaborate coloratura without stopping for breath, and there are few pentimenti.

Out of its web, topsy-turvy, emerge suggestions of features which range from the anthropomorphic to the monstrous. In the lower left Miró collaged the head of a smiling lady in an elegant hat that he contrasted near the top with a gentleman's hat, also collaged. There is no head under this hat, but above it Miró drew the head of a monster gnashing its teeth. In the center, where the arabesques suggest a skeletal figure, the image is topped with a skull cut from a medical textbook. Flying above the metamorphosed "personage" on the right is a collaged machine with a bird's head—a parsing, as it were, of a favorite Miró image, the bird-airplane (which goes back all the way to *The Hunter*, p. 23).

DRAWING-COLLAGE. *1933. Charcoal, pencil, wash, and decal, 25¼ x 17⅛ inches. (C&N, p. 125)*

Though dating from the same period as the collages with postcards, the drawing of this figure—indeed the entire conception—is purposely more awkward and more overtly humorous.

Although Miró requested in 1968 that the title of this work be changed from *L'Origine de la bête humaine* to its present simple form, *Drawing-Collage*, the prior title does offer some hints as to a possible iconography for this curious figure. The explicit rendering of the phallus and the prominence of the closed eye, the breasts upon the lozenge-shaped form rising from the torso, in combination with the connotations of generation and primordial beginnings suggested by the collaged chick newly emerged from its egg and the eellike fish shooting up from the sea, may be read as a whimsical interpretation of the legend of Adam and Eve. The forms themselves suggest primitive scaffoldings of bone and flesh not unlike the limbs of Picasso's fantastical bathers of the Dinard period.

In its morphology, although certainly not in its light and amused spirit, this collage anticipates Miró's *tableaux sauvages* of the succeeding years.

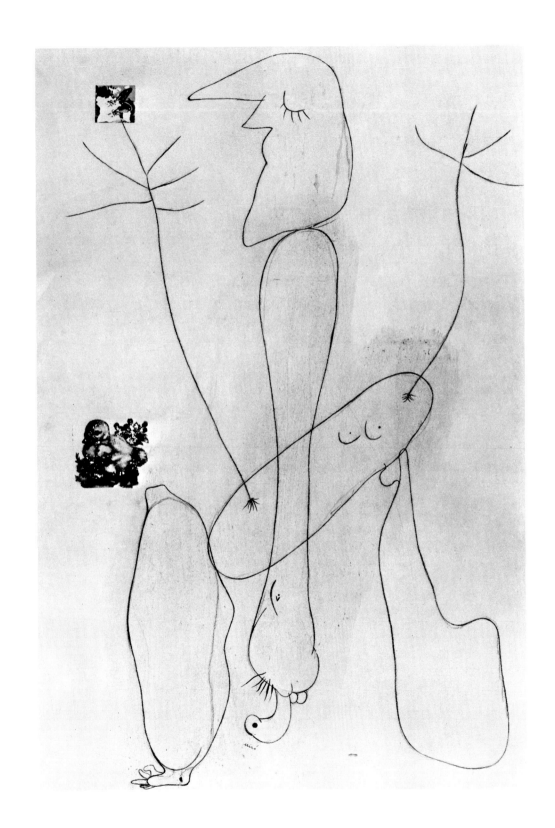

HIRONDELLE / AMOUR.[1] *Winter 1933–34. Oil on canvas, 6 feet 6½ inches x 8 feet 1½ inches. (C&N, p. 125)*

This large painting is Miró's consummate masterpiece. No other single work contains so much of him, in such perfect equilibrium. Never since has he handled the big picture with greater breadth or abandon. His color here is at its most effulgent and its most artless; its exquisitely calibrated orchestration depends less on variety—the gamut is virtually limited to black, white, and the primaries—than on quantification and disposition.

Hirondelle / Amour ("Swallow / Love") is one of four paintings of 1934 that were occasioned by a commission for a group of tapestry cartoons.[2] In executing these pictures, however, Miró made no concession to the techniques of the weaver and conceived them entirely as paintings in their own right. The painting is the product of a more spontaneous procedure than had been used the previous year for the large paintings based on collages (p. 60). The drawing, though less "automatic" than in certain 1925–26 paintings, not only recaptures the spontaneity of that era, but exhibits greater exuberance and rhythmic continuity—and this within an overall context of more commanding pictorial authority. The forms seem to spill from Miró's brush as it figure-skates its way across the blue ground which we read as sky. Most of the illusionist space of the 1933 paintings has disappeared. No longer isolated in static suspension but galvanized by continuous rhythms, the now slightly shaded design elements are locked into the picture plane in reciprocal relation to the blue ground, so that the configuration binds the entire surface.

Miró's hand seems to reenact the ecstasy of flight. Among the figures that tumble from it as it glides across the canvas is a swallow; without lifting the brush dipped in the black of his contour lines, he writes the word *hirondelle*. Just below, in a free association to his sensations of joy, freedom, and simple celerity, he writes *amour*. Functioning as decorative linear passages as well as poetic allusions, these words recall the graphism of Miró's "picture-poems" of the twenties,[3] except that here the words are not set in syntactical arrangements but function rather as simple exclamations.

It is impossible to identify most of the shapes in *Hirondelle / Amour* as specific motifs. At the bottom, to be sure, there is the suggestion of a human head juxtaposed helter-skelter with stylized signs that in Miró's other paintings often stand for breasts and for hair. And at the top—swooping, hovering, darting—is unquestionably a flock of birds. In between, however, seeming to rise from the constraints of gravity and aspiring to the weightlessness and freedom of flight, are forms which suggest human limbs that alternately issue into hands or feet—or metamorphose into birds. It was probably with regard to pictures such as *Hirondelle / Amour* that Giacometti, one of Miró's closest friends at the time it was painted, was later to say, "For me, Miró was synonymous with freedom—something more aerial, more liberated, lighter than anything I had ever seen before."[4]

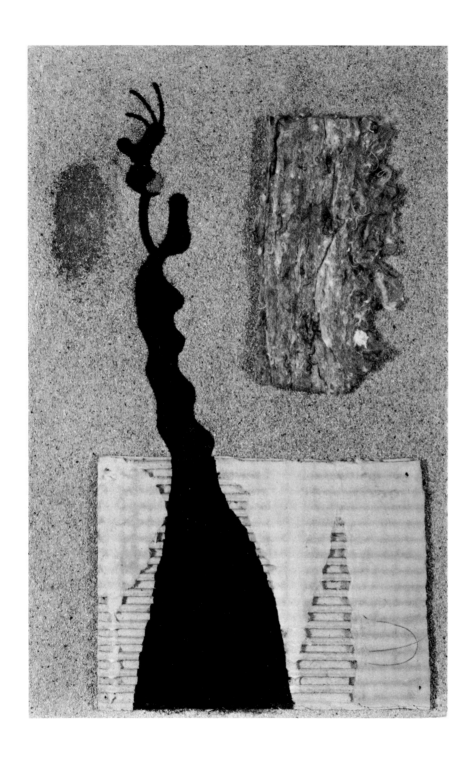

COLLAGE. *January 1934. Collage on sandpaper, 14⅝ x 9⅜ inches. (C&N, p. 126)*

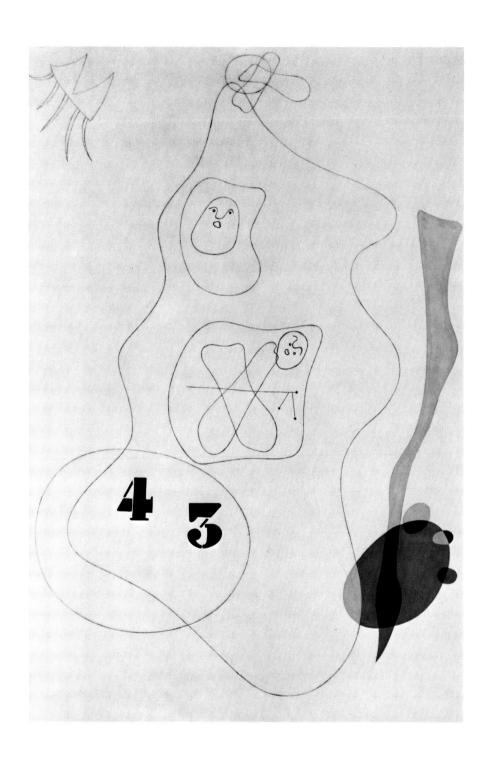

GOUACHE-DRAWING. *August 1934. Gouache and pencil on paper, 42 x 28 inches. (C&N, p. 126)*

tion of his mature style. So intense is the chiaroscuro of the creatures that, like many of Picasso's bathers of 1929–30, they almost seem studies for sculptures.

In many images in this series the modeling serves to intensify conceptions of the body that suggest strain, even agony. In that context, the *Opera Singer* is something of an exception, even though a certain sense of discomfort is produced by the asymmetrical head and twisted mouth. The calligraphy on the sheet the singer holds, which stands "more or less for music," her single toenail, her tuft of pubic hair, and, above all, what Miró has identified as her buttocks—formed of two tiny black balls—all belong to the droll vocabulary of Miró's earlier work.

ROPE AND PEOPLE I. *March 1935. Oil on cardboard mounted on wood, with coil of rope, 41¼ x 29⅜ inches. (C&N, p. 127)*

Perhaps no example of Miró's *tableaux sauvages* is richer in its implications than this rope collage. Whereas the protruding nails of the *Relief Construction* (p. 53) endowed an otherwise formal relief with a disturbing overtone of potential aggression, the rope here establishes an iconography of cruelty and violence that is sustained in the gestures and expressions of the figures themselves. Miró began by nailing the rope, especially chosen for its roughness, to the cardboard support. The three personages he painted around it—a man to the left, a young girl and a woman to the right—were suggested by association with the rope, which he saw as "binding and torturing them." The emotional ambience of the picture is one in which the author and his creatures seem already racked by the tensions which would shortly break out in the form of the Spanish Civil War.

The projecting noses and sawtooth, naillike dentures of the two adults are characteristic of the *tableaux sauvages*. And if the drawing still retains a note of Miróesque whimsy, it takes the form of *humour noir*. The man bites his own hand in a motif that recalls the inward-turned aggressions of figures in the Romanesque manuscripts that Miró loves so well. It also confirms that the violence is not only from without, and that the rope is thus also a metaphor for an inner anger and anxiety that constricts and convulses the figures.

OPERA SINGER. *October 1934. Pastel, 41⅜ x 29⅛ inches. (C&N, p. 126)*

The earliest phase of what Miró was to call his *tableaux sauvages*—"wild pictures"—was a series of fifteen pastels executed at Montroig in the summer of 1934. Gone were the cursive drawing and brilliant flat colors of such pictures of the previous winter as *Hirondelle / Amour*. Instead of using pastel to dissolve contours and disembody forms, as did Degas and Redon, Miró reversed the traditional process in these figures and modeled the forms with more relief and solidity than at any time since the incep-

OBJECT. *Barcelona, spring 1936. Construction of hollowed wooden post, stuffed parrot on wooden stand, hat, and map, 31⅛ inches high x 11⅞ inches wide x 10¼ inches deep. (C&N, p. 127)*

This object is distinguished from Miró's other constructions, earlier and later, by its more thoroughgoing literary character, which placed it more directly in the spirit of the Surrealist objects that proliferated in avant-garde circles during the 1930s. Elsewhere, Miró tended to shape or paint over the *objets trouvés* he used; here all the components save the wooden cylinder (cut by a carpenter according to the artist's specifications) were used as found.

The Surrealist object was essentially a three-dimensional collage of found articles chosen for their metaphoric potential rather than for their purely visual, that is plastic, value. Its literary character opened the possibility of its fabrication – or, better, its confection – to poets, critics, and others who stood, professionally speaking, outside or on the margins of the plastic arts. This partially explains the tremendous vogue that reached a climax in the famous "Exposition Surréaliste d'Objets" held in Paris at the Charles Ratton Gallery in May 1936. The flurry of activity leading to that exhibition seems to have inspired Miró to create this very uncharacteristic work in Barcelona during the spring of the year.

The principle underlying the Surrealist object was not new, to be sure. Duchamp had provided the most important prototype in his "assisted" Readymades of 1920–21, such as *Why Not Sneeze?* (fig. 51). These, of course, depended in turn on the liberties established by Picasso in his Cubist constructions. However, in the Picassos, the poetic implications of the constituent elements were subordinate to the formal syntax of the whole. Duchamp attempted rather to use these found materials in a wholly nonplastic way, subjecting them to the same kind of *dépaysement* – dissociation or displacement – as that to which the Symbolist poets had subjected words in an attempt to liberate their hidden meanings.[1] For Duchamp, the selection of Readymade objects "was never dictated by an esthetic delectation. The choice was based on a reaction of visual *indifference . . .* in fact, a complete anesthesia."[2] Not long after Duchamp's *démarche*, André Breton suggested "the concrete realization and subsequent circulation of objects . . . perceived only in dreams."[3] His call went unheeded at that time, however, and it was only after 1930 that object art flourished in avant-garde circles;

its efflorescence was simultaneous with the vogue of *trompe-l'œil* illusionism that marked the new goals of Surrealist painting.[4] The Surrealist heroes of the twenties had either left the movement (Masson), drifted to its periphery (Miró), or adopted more illusionist styles (Ernst). The realistically imaged but oneirically combined objects in the paintings of Magritte and Dali – the prototypical Surrealist painters of the thirties – provided an immediate context for the Surrealist objects.

Miró's 1936 object may be read – and Miró concurs with this interpretation – as a kind of poetic fantasy, a chain of associations literally springing from the head of the man whose hat forms the base of the construction. Thus, the red plastic fish that swims around the brim of the latter and the map[5] that projects from it suggest the vast expanses of the mind's universe. The isolation of a lady's gartered leg, her foot in an elegant high-heeled shoe, focuses interest on a very particular region of the subject's thoughts. This fetishistically isolated leg is actually movable, as it hangs from a string; it thus echoes Dali's famous *Object of Symbolic Function* of 1931 (fig. 52), which contained images of high-heeled shoes, one of them suspended by a string.[6]

Placed in apposition to the woman's leg in Miró's object, and also hanging from a string, is a small ball. Given the context, we would probably not be wrong in attributing a sexual connotation to the latter. Certainly it brings to mind one of Giacometti's most famous objects, the *Suspended Ball*, 1930–31 (fig. 53), well known to Miró and, from the outset, in the collection of André Breton, who made much of its cryptosexual functioning.[7] Finally, the string supporting the ball in Miró's object hangs from the oval base of a phallic-looking limb that supports a green parrot, later to reappear as the bird of love.[8]

In this object, Miró was working a terrain that was not properly his own. Though a poetic painter, he is not a literary artist of the type that can entirely put aside plastic concerns. Indeed, to the extent that the wooden core of his work was carefully designed, Miró did not even try to put them aside. Moreover, sculpture does not separate itself as clearly as does painting from the world of objects. Almost any three-dimensional form can be *seen as sculpture*, if not necessarily as good sculpture. The determination is largely based on the observer's expectations or mental set (both related, of course, to context). After years of assimilation of objects into sculpture, even many of the intendedly anti-aesthetic Readymades of Duchamp have taken on an inescapably "arty" look. However much Miró may have tried to minimize his aesthetic consciousness in putting together the Museum's object, it is precisely the presence of his formative hand that makes this work enduring, that keeps it interesting after many cleverer and more *outré* objects by his Surrealist friends have begun to pall.

AIDEZ L'ESPAGNE. *1937. Stencil, printed in color (from Cahiers d'Art, vol. 12, no. 4–5, 1937), 9¾ x 7⅝ inches. (C&N, p. 128)*

STILL LIFE WITH OLD SHOE. *Paris, January–May 1937. Oil on canvas, 32¼ x 46 inches. (C&N, p. 128)*

The tragic realism of this picture has little in common, affectively or stylistically, with the realism of Miró's work prior to 1924. It emerged suddenly in 1937—Miró worked on *Still Life with Old Shoe* from late January through May of that year—and appeared only once again, in the hallucinated *Self-Portrait* of 1938. It marks a momentary crisis in Miró's conception of himself, his art, and the latter's relation to the public.

Miró had never displayed an interest in politics, but the fratricidal Spanish Civil War forced him to take sides. The artist was "almost sick with anxiety,"[1] and, as was the case with Picasso, the tragedy not only profoundly touched his consciousness, but momentarily redirected his art. *The Reaper* (fig. 54), the large mural painted for the Spanish pavilion of the Paris World's Fair of 1937, is generally considered Miró's counterpart to Picasso's *Guernica*, likewise commissioned for that pavilion. As did *Guernica*, *The Reaper* dealt with current events through symbolic allusion. More manifestly *engagé* was Miró's poster *Aidez l'Espagne* (left), which shows a figure wearing what appears to be a Catalan *barreta* giving the clenched-fist Loyalist salute. Miró's inscription on the poster, however, clearly indicates the elevated, almost suprapolitical tone of his commitment: "In the present struggle I see, on the Fascist side, spent forces; on the opposite side, the people, whose boundless creative will gives Spain an impetus which will astonish the world."

The most profound counterpart to *Guernica* in Miró's œuvre is this modest *Still Life with Old Shoe*, in which Miró spells out his sense of "the people" by transfiguring a group of their humble possessions. These are juxtaposed not on a table as in a conventional still life, but in a bleak landscape oppressed by a sky in which an ominous shadow floats in on the left, while the black clouds which converge on the right mingle with "the sinister colours of a great conflagration."[2] The darkness, tragic in connotation, is mitigated by clusters of pure color which seem to emanate from within the inanimate objects—as if Miró's brush had suddenly revealed their potential spiritual content.

The almost disconcerting intrusion of realism into Miró's style at this point in his career was a function of many concerns. Like other great modern painters, Miró had created a personal visual language that could be easily read only by those familiar with advanced twentieth-cen-

tury painting. It seems certain that during the war that racked Spain Miró questioned whether his art, so beyond the comprehension of all but a few of his countrymen, was sufficiently in the service of their humanity. It was not that he was interested in particular causes or serving the ends of political propaganda; but the desire to communicate more readily, an aim that led some artists of his generation to Social Realism, was surely in his mind.

Indeed, Miró's painting had never been—nor would it ever be—wholly abstract; however summary or elliptical his symbols, they always referred to something concrete. During the early thirties, however, his private sign language had become even more remote from nature than it had earlier been—hence more difficult to read. And it is

therefore not surprising that the crisis which led to Miró's return to realism in *Still Life with Old Shoe* should have been anticipated by a return to sketching from the model. This Miró had already begun in the summer of 1936, side by side with the students at the Académie de la Grande Chaumière. The realism of *Still Life with Old Shoe* thus culminated plastically as well as thematically the rediscovery of his roots, and constituted a not unexpected reflex in a period when the artist could hardly bring himself to paint, and when, it has even been argued, his imagination was "running dry." [3]

The execution of *Still Life with Old Shoe* may be thought of as a ritualistic recapitulation of Miró's mastery of the primary materials of his art, and it is clear that its successful realization profoundly reassured the painter. Miró actually set up the objects—an apple[4] with a fork plunged into it, a partially wrapped gin bottle (the letters GI . . . are visible just below its neck), a broken loaf of bread, and an old shoe—on a table of the mezzanine of the Pierre Loeb gallery.[5] He came in almost every day for a month to paint, then moved his assembly of objects to a studio he had just taken on the Rue Blanqui—where he continued to work on the canvas for another four months.

It has often been observed that the inclusion of the old shoe is reminiscent of van Gogh.[6] The Dutch painter was one of Miró's favorites in his early years, and Miró certainly wished to express here a van Gogh–like solidarity with those who live close to the earth. But, in this instance, the analogy with van Gogh goes beyond the inclusion of a shoe as such and touches on the whole psychology of picture-making. When van Gogh felt most psychologically unsure, when his grip on the world about him was loosened, he often found that by isolating a few objects—a pipe on a chair, for example—and carefully painting them, he could regain his equilibrium. Representational painting is, after all, a form of recapitulation of one's knowledge of—hence one's grip on—the world of objects, and such paintings certainly constituted a form of therapy for van Gogh.[7] In his letters he speaks of the feeling of calm and well-being that followed the making of such a painting. Not that Miró needed reassurance on anything like the same level, but his return to realism in this picture, to those objects that for the previous twelve years had been indicated by elliptical and often ambiguous signs, was certainly a function of psychological as well as social distress and anxiety. The closing in on the objects—especially in the absence of a familiar still-life context—endows them with an unexpected and disquieting scale, and stresses their importance to the painter. There is something distinctly obsessional about *Still Life with Old Shoe* beyond the fact of the months of painstaking work Miró lavished on it.

HEAD OF A MAN. *Montroig, summer 1937. Gouache and India ink on black paper, 25⅝ x 19¾ inches. (C&N, p. 129)*

So pervasively gentle is Miró's nature that many of the *tableaux sauvages* of the 1930s fail to convince us of his anger. What begins as ferocity often seems to soften into humor—expressed through a tendency toward caricature in the contouring of the features. *Head of a Man* is one of those *tableaux sauvages* that utterly convince; it is a picture in which the pressure of Miró's anger is most relentless.

That pressure is first felt in the extraordinary contouring of the immense head that surges from the narrow neck to fill the pictorial field almost to its edges. Its silhouette has the quality of being found, point by point, as Miró's brush moves along the surface. None of the features in the outer contour—the nose that descends to close the mouth like an overhanging lip, the protruding forehead, the rear-bumper ear—fall into the patterns or formulations for facial features already familiar in Miró's work. These freshly conceived lineaments combine to produce a violence of expression comparable to that of Picasso's *Guernica* period. Indeed, the Mirós and Picassos in question are contemporary, sharing the anguish of the most terrible period in the Spanish Civil War.

In *Head of a Man* the contours of the head enclose an area of apparently random blottings and splotches of thinned-out medium—stainings of red, blue, purple, green, brown, and other colors. The area outside the profile is a gloomy and largely opaque gray-black. Indeed, through the choice of a black paper, Miró reversed his usual approach to figure and ground (see pp. 31, 58, 80), in which the figure is opaque and the surrounding space is painterly or atmospheric. The inversion here reinforces the expressiveness of the conceit by making the seemingly impenetrable world around the figure appear to lock him in. At the same time, the stained passages suggest (in an entirely nonliteral way) the interiority of the flesh—as if we were somehow permitted to see below surface appearances.

To the extent that the stained passages suggest the inner body and thus tissues, body fluids, and the like, the surface may be imagined as a kind of litmus paper on which liquid containing primordial monocellular forms of life has been deposited. Such a reading is in keeping with the character of the eye of the figure, which looks like an antediluvian creature crawling through the primeval slime. A round, delicate, and diaphanous organism, it is threatened by the opaque and jagged trap formed by the figure's mouth and teeth. Allusions to the microscopic are a continuing aspect of Miró's poetic battery, and follow naturally from a commitment to biomorphism. They give an appropriate atavistic and primitive dimension to the angry and anguished expression in *Head of a Man*.

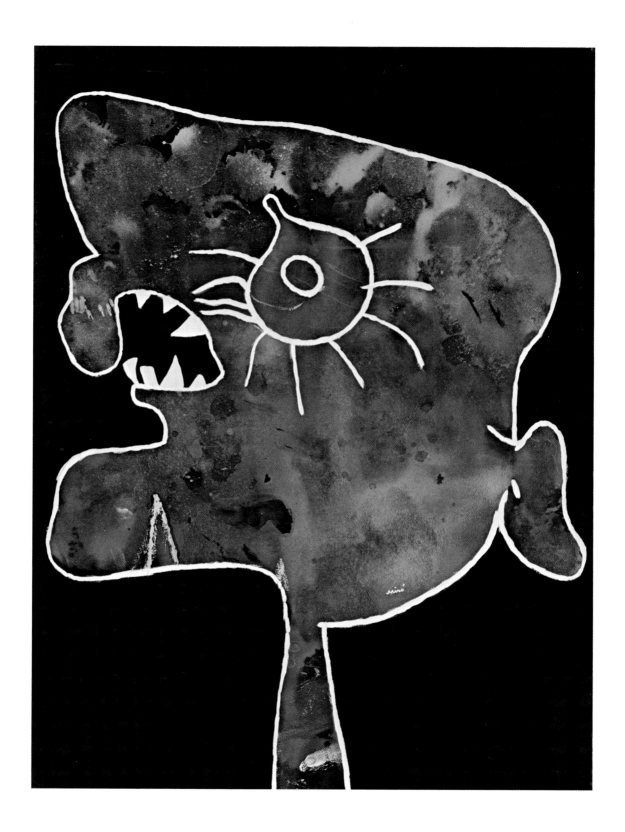

SELF-PORTRAIT I. *Paris, 1937–38. Pencil, crayon, and oil on canvas, 57½ x 38¼ inches. (C&N, p. 129)*

Miró's interrogation of the world of objects in *Still Life with Old Shoe* led quite naturally to a consideration of the manner in which he understood and experienced objects, that is, to the workings of his own mind. It is not surprising, therefore, that toward the end of 1937 he explored his own thought processes in an extraordinary *Self-Portrait*, his first in twenty years. The picture has been aptly characterized as an "examination of conscience"[1] and an act "of self-criticism."[2]

This is certainly one of the most revelatory images any artist has ever made of himself. It is also one of the greatest drawings in the modernist tradition. Although executed on canvas, its forms heightened here and there with touches of diluted oil paint, the image is almost entirely formed by penciled lines and shading. Miró had actually intended to make an oil painting, but the drawing seemed to realize so completely his sense of himself that he could not bear to paint over it. The picture has therefore been referred to as "unfinished,"[3] but it is unfinished only in the sense that Picasso's *Girl with a Mandolin* and *Charnel House* are—in the manner of Columbus's voyage to the Orient.

Had Miró painted over the drawing, it is hard to imagine that the colors of his palette could have communicated the elusive, delicately shaded regions of the psyche as effectively as do the exquisitely nuanced grays that we see. (Miró did, in fact, realize the project as a painting by using a facsimile, but only much later.)[4]

The point of departure for *Self-Portrait* was the same searching realism as in *Still Life with Old Shoe*. Here again, Miró worked from the motif. In a little room in his apartment on the Rue Blanqui he set up his easel and a round convex mirror. He worked painstakingly, repeatedly glancing at his reflected image. It has been observed that the distortion of the convex mirror probably contributed something to the looming effect of the image.[5] But the latter is fundamentally the result of an aesthetic and expressive choice. Indeed, Miró would have had to want that effect in choosing a convex mirror in the first place.

The monumental effect of *Self-Portrait* is a function more of scale than of actual size. Miró's head seems to tower over us partially because of the way in which his bust presses up to the picture plane and crowds the field of the canvas laterally. Comparison with the *Self-Portrait* of 1919 in Picasso's collection (fig. 58) shows how the space between Miró and the viewer has evaporated. In the earlier work the bust is comfortably situated within the frame and the head sufficiently recessed to open up a psychological as well as physical distance between the viewer and the viewed.

The *Self-Portrait* of 1937 begins with a stylized rendering of Miró's features not unlike the contouring of the 1919 image. The latter was probably influenced, in its drawing, by Romanesque frescoes;[6] but only in the later image was Miró open to the fantastical aspect of that art. Both pictures contain the same self-consciously pursed lips, flared nostrils, and out-turned ears. In the earlier work, however, Miró gives us but a skin-deep self-image, whereas in the later he has rendered himself transparent. From out of the contours of his features emerges the universe of his imagination. His liberated line has woven a galactic tracery of sparks, flames, suns, and stars—an apocalypse worthy of the Romanesque. This astral conflagration seems to begin in the incandescent eyes and to pass with incendiary rapidity throughout the space of the image. The real features seem almost to dissolve into the swirling chiaroscuro, as if "all impurities [had] been burned away."[7] What remains are *les étincelles*, the sparks of pure idea, the single cells from which *miromonde* grew, bodied forth in Miró's iconography through a variety of references to light—from a firefly to a sun to the shimmering of a thousand sardines.

Beginning as a realistic drawing of the artist's face and ending as an epiphany of his private universe, this work seems to have reconfirmed for Miró the authenticity of that universe. For it is with *Self-Portrait* that the period of crisis comes to an end and Miró resumes his personal style with a new vigor. *Self-Portrait II* (fig. 59), executed later in the year (1938) that saw the completion of *Self-Portrait I*, retains only the two flaming eyes—as if the painter had reduced himself to his essential organ. The rest of that picture is once again pure *miromonde*.

SEATED WOMAN I.[1] *Paris, December 1938. Oil on canvas, 64⅜ x 51⅛ inches. (C&N, p. 130)*

This first of a remarkable pair of seated women was completed by Miró in December 1938; the second (fig. 60) dates from two months later. Both show a lady with an extraordinarily long neck gesturing with hands raised; both also have a roughly oval sun overlapping a rectangular window in the upper right of the canvas. But there the resemblances end. In the Museum's picture, the large, simply contoured, and almost relentlessly flat forms play host to pure colors of a saturation beyond anything posited in Miró's earlier work. *Seated Woman II*, on the other hand, is an intricately composed and expressively violent picture—the last of Miró's *tableaux sauvages*—and is organized primarily in terms of light and dark rather than through the juxtaposition of pure hues.

The antecedents of *Seated Woman I* are to be found in such pictures as *Portrait of Mistress Mills in 1750*, 1929 (p. 48). But one has only to compare the two pictures to see how Miró has sacrificed intricacy in the interests of breadth, ornament in the interests of boldness. The signs of Miró's familiar whimsy are nonetheless still present. The head floats like a red balloon attached to the neck by a linear string, and the breasts and hands are drolly minuscule in relation to the giant torso. The sex, preposterously enlarged, is analogized to the red disks of the head and the sun—which is secondarily alluded to through the similarity of the pubic hair to Miró's earlier sign for solar irradiation.[2]

Yet none of this is as central to the experience of the picture as its purely sensory impact. We respond immediately to the contrast of the rich yellow wall and the airily painted Prussian blue skirt, both riveted to the picture plane by disks of saturated red. In contrast to *Woman II* with its convoluted if brilliantly tortured silhouettes, the Museum's picture is notable for its air of genial awkwardness and its direct, uncomplicated effects.

THE BEAUTIFUL BIRD REVEALING[1] THE UNKNOWN TO A PAIR OF LOVERS. *Montroig, July 1941. Gouache and oil wash, 18 x 15 inches. (C&N, p. 131)*

The Beautiful Bird Revealing the Unknown to a Pair of Lovers is the twenty-first in the series of twenty-three "Constellations" executed between January 1940 and September 1941 in Varengeville-sur-Mer (nos. 1–10), Palma de Mallorca (11–20), and Montroig (21–23). These works constitute a series "in the highest sense of the term," as André Breton has pointed out;[2] certainly their common properties are more consistent than in any earlier groups of Miró's works referred to as series. Not only does the ambience in each work remain the same — firmaments teeming with suns, stars, birds, lovers — but all the works are executed in the same medium (oil wash and gouache) on same-size sheets of paper.

The particulars of the style are consistent also. Flat opaque shapes of pure color executed in gouache and connected by a linear tracery are suspended in front of delicately modulated grounds. The gouache is applied with obsessional precision and there are no pentimenti. The grounds are achieved by spreading oil wash on moistened paper, scraped to bring out its texture. "The hand engages in patient operations of rubbing, abrading, impregnating, massaging into life variously pigmented, variously somber or transparent gleams over the entire surface, realizing imperceptible transitions from one color to another or blending them in a single misty cloud."[3] The resulting grounds suggest a nebulous, indeterminate space in front of which the flat, precisely contoured gouache motifs hang like a curtain defining the picture plane.

There is, however, one crucial feature, the nature of the configuration, that is not common to all the Constellations. The multiplication of small motifs spotted over the surface in an "allover" manner as in *The Beautiful Bird*, the very clustering of minuscule accents that suggested to Miró the generic name "Constellations," did not appear until the tenth gouache in the series, dated May 14, 1940. Nevertheless, it is this configuration that is the most important plastic contribution of this series — indeed, of all Miró's later work — to the development of post–World War II painting. The allover articulation evolved out of the process of painting itself. "I would set out with no preconceived idea," Miró recalls. "A few forms suggested here would call for other forms elsewhere to balance them. These in turn demanded others. It seemed intermin-

able...I would take [a gouache] up day after day to paint in other tiny spots, stars, washes, infinitesimal dots of color in order finally to achieve a full and complex equilibrium."[4]

In order to shift the focus of interest from individual forms to the matrix that binds them, Miró tended to simplify his language. In *The Beautiful Bird*, there are few of his familiar meandering biomorphic forms, and most of these are not filled in, so that their arabesques lose themselves visually in the labyrinth of the composition. By contrast, the flat gouache shapes that spring toward the eye are all variants or sections of very simple geometries — circles, squares, ovals, triangles, crescents, etc. These are interesting in terms of their collective density and rhythm rather than as individual forms.

In *The Beautiful Bird*, as in the other fully developed, hence later Constellations of the series, traditional compositional hierarchies are undermined by the carefully controlled "allover" dosing. Spacing is fairly regular; there are no large empty spaces — one might almost speak of *horror vacui*. By the same token there are no dominant clusters, and there is little overlapping. It is not surprising that, as Miró has affirmed, the original idea for the twinkling configuration of such Constellations was suggested by reflections on water.[5] As a motif, water provides flickering highlights on a surface constantly in motion, a surface of a substance that, like the space of the Constellations, is of indeterminate depth and density. Twenty-seven years earlier water had furnished Mondrian with the point of departure for his not unrelated allover "plus-and-minus" pictures, which were extrapolated from pier and ocean motifs. Indeed, it may be said that while Miró did not have these Mondrians in mind, the very same motif which even earlier had given the Impressionists the taste for an atomized field of sensations had led Miró, in effect, to take up the allover conception where it had been left in late Analytic Cubism, and to convert it from rectilinear into curvilinear terms (thus providing, as it happened, a more immediate and congenial model for some young American painters of the forties).

The importance of the Constellations to the development of American painting after 1945 can hardly be overestimated. They were the first works by a major European artist that were seen in New York after World War II (except, of course, for those by artists who had fled to America). When they were shown at the Pierre Matisse Gallery in 1945, just two years before Pollock "broke the ice" for

American painters with his own version of the allover configuration, the Constellations aroused tremendous enthusiasm, especially among avant-garde artists.

As with Mondrian's "plus-and-minus" compositions and Pollock's classic poured pictures, the allover articulation of the later Constellations constitutes only what may be called the "prior condition" of the configurations. Slight variations *from* such implicit regularity are precisely what in fact animates each composition. These variations solicit careful looking; we become aware of the subtle hierarchies of size and number, of the piquant variations in tone and density of the ground, and are struck all the more by the unexpected interstitial flash of a pure color—such as the red of the sex of the woman at the right in *The Beautiful Bird*.

Reference, at this point, to the readability of motifs in *The Beautiful Bird* may surprise the reader. So predominantly abstract do the Constellations appear that one is likely to overlook Miró's poetic personages, who are very much present, however camouflaged they may be through absorption into the decorative patterning. While Miró's seemingly metaphoric poetic titles are added after the completion of the picture, so that the latter can in no way be considered an "illustration" of a prior conceit, the relation between image and title is more direct than appears at first glance. In *The Beautiful Bird Revealing the Unknown to a Pair of Lovers*, for example, the entities named are all discernible. The bird flies in on the upper right. Its disproportionately large head has a parrotlike beak echoed in form by its pointed tongue, the black shape of which is repeated, in turn, by the black lid of the bird's eye. The line connecting the head to the fanlike tail is interrupted by two tiny disks of the kind that dot the painting throughout. This, combined with the fact that the tail is one half of the "hourglass"[6] form that is repeated all over the surface, tends to submerge the image of the bird in the abstract decorative pattern—betokening a universe more insubstantial than in Miró's anterior work.

Not quite so elusive as the bird is the figure of the buxom female sitting at the lower right. Her body is spotted with little disks and hourglass forms of varying sizes, and certain details, such as her double necklace (very similar to that of the *Seated Woman*, p. 79), are composed of the same disks and lines that make up the allover tracery. But other features of hers are unique. These include her awesome red and black vagina (the "bold formal sign which Miró uses to designate the vulva")[7] and her buttocks, defined by a large black double-crescent. The latter tends to be read secondarily as a mouth, to the extent that the targetlike breasts also suggest—in conjunction with the sex—the features of a face. Standing to the left of this mammoth woman, whose snoutlike nose rises as if to scent the bird above, is her pint-sized lover, whose most distinguishing features are the lumps extruding hairs on his nose and forehead.

Beyond the bird and lovers cited in the title, there are few other distinguishable motifs in *The Beautiful Bird*. Above the man's head we see a snail inching its way toward a crescent moon; a little ladder to the sky (see p. 24) is discernible just under the body of the bird, and stars are visible near the lower left and upper right corners. But the greater part of the image is given over to a play of simple quasi-geometrical shapes, varied in size, shape, and number and juxtaposed or chained together in improvised sequences. Miró has referred to these constellations of shapes as "musical space fillers," and it is logical that he should draw his metaphor for such effects from the most abstract of the arts. Indeed, the multiplicity of little black accents of varying sizes and related shapes are almost analogous to the quavers, semiquavers, demisemiquavers, and hemidemisemiquavers of musical notation. *The Beautiful Bird* contains analogies to arpeggiated effects, glissandi, and a whole range of rhythms, all of which are orchestrated within the nuanced sensibility of chamber music. Such Constellations do indeed *atenuar la música*—"attain to music"[8]—an injunction Miró had inscribed in a sketchbook several years earlier. Miró himself tells us that the abstract spirit of the Constellations was directly related to his experience of the private, nonparticularized language of music. "I felt a deep desire to escape," Miró said of this period some time later. "I closed within myself purposely. The night, music and stars began to play a major role in suggesting my paintings. Music had always appealed to me, and now music in this period began to take the role poetry had played in the early twenties—especially Bach and Mozart, when I went back to Majorca upon the fall of France."[9]

PAINTING. *1950. Oil on canvas, 32 x 39½ inches. (C&N, p. 131)*

PORTRAIT OF A MAN IN A LATE NINETEENTH CENTURY FRAME.[1] *1950.[2] Oil on canvas with ornamented wood frame, 57½ x 49¼ inches (including frame). (C&N, p. 131)*

Miró's childhood friend Juan Prats, once a student of painting and later Barcelona's leading haberdasher, came upon this preposterously framed, pompous memorial portrait and sent it to the artist as a joke. The sitter is the epitome of the self-satisfied, pious, *bien-pensant* bourgeois; his pose and costume, the official medal and ribbon on his table, the religious pictures on the table and wall, and the rose garden visible through the window all allude to the secure, self-assured universe in which he functioned.

The deceased gentleman seems absorbed in lofty thought, his eyes directed heavenward. Possibly he is engrossed in complacent contemplation of a deservedly well-ordered afterlife. Into this vision, superimposed on the reassuring objects of the sitter's comfortable surroundings, Miró has mischievously inserted an unsettling dose of the unexpected and irrational—emblems of the unconscious and heralds of the unknown. As if to suggest the sitter's confusion at this unwonted interruption, Miró drew on his forehead a coil pattern, rather like a broken spring. Imaged on the rose garden seen through the window at the upper right are configurations familiar to us from the Constellations (p. 80): in the upper right is the sign Miró uses to designate the vulva, and to the left are two long vertical and three short horizontal parallel lines enclosing little boxes of brilliant color on which is superimposed an arabesque. In its resemblance to the treble clef, the latter makes the whole passage seem a kind of whimsical musical calligraphy—no doubt related to the singing of the bird.

The whole ambience has, indeed, been altered. By scraping away the paint around the sitter, Miró produced a suggestion of vague, unmeasurable space that, like a cloud of malaise, envelops the solid bourgeois. This space is totally at odds with the ordered illusionism of the original— determined as it was by precise coordinates—and derives ultimately from the atmospheric space of Miró's fantasy pictures of the mid-twenties.

Suspended in front of this space, situated on the picture plane itself, are a group of Miróesque symbols—the forms in the garden, a sharp-toothed little monster approaching the sitter on the lower right, a horned grotesque flying between the sitter's head and a blue cloud, and, below, a red disk with a white halo. All these signs appear to have been suddenly made manifest as if the picture plane were a kind of x-ray put before the sitter's conventional world, a visionary x-ray that reveals the metaphysical forces actually at work (much in the manner of Duchamp's *Large Glass*, whose "fourth-dimensional" forms are suspended against the vista of the real world seen through the glass).

MURAL PAINTING. *Barcelona, 1950–51. Oil on canvas, 6 feet 2¾ inches x 19 feet 5¾ inches. (C&N, p. 132)*

Except for the lost *Reaper* (fig. 54), made for a stairway landing of the Spanish pavilion at the Paris World's Fair of 1937, it was only after World War II that Miró had the occasion to execute wall-size paintings. In 1947 he was commissioned to do a 31½-foot mural to decorate the Gourmet Restaurant of the Terrace Hilton Hotel in Cincinnati. Then, in 1950, at the suggestion of architect Walter Gropius, Harvard University commissioned the mural, now at The Museum of Modern Art, for the Harkness Commons building of the graduate center. Whereas Miró had come to America to realize the Cincinnati commission—he had rented a studio in New York City for that purpose—the Harvard mural was approved on the basis of a sketch (fig. 62) and executed in Barcelona in the winter of 1950–51. The large oil on canvas was set into the wall of the dining room of Harkness Commons (fig. 63) later in 1951.

In the ensuing years it turned out to be exceedingly difficult to keep the picture clean, and experts from the University's Fogg Art Museum found that it was deteriorating. During a visit to Harvard in the late 1950s Miró proposed that the mural be replaced by a ceramic version of the same composition, and this was effected in 1960. The painting was acquired by the Museum in 1963.

In making this large mural, Miró wrote that he "wanted to work with the plastic rigor and the élan of the great Romanesque frescoes of our Barcelona museum."[1] But, while Miró equaled the simplicity and stunning decorative power of those medieval frescoes in *Mural Painting*, he made no attempt to assimilate their particular qualities of design and color. Indeed, the color and drawing of many Miró paintings of the twenties are closer to the Romanesque than is *Mural Painting*. Its achievement represented not a new exploration, but a successful transposition to a wall-size work of a stylistic formula common in Miró's smaller pictures even before the period of the Constellations. Against a soft and atmospheric ground of subtly shifting hues, figures are contoured in black; some of these are filled in with patterns in opaque flat colors—usually the primaries—or black; others remain "transparent," the ground colors showing through. Miró alluded to this when he wrote the Museum in March 1964 that *Mural Painting* was "highly representative," a "capital work [which] summed up all my research."[2]

Miró identifies the motifs of *Mural Painting* simply as a bull and figures; he cryptically described the subject as "of a muralistic and poetic significance."[3] Indeed, the motifs have tended to be viewed by writers on Miró primarily as "pretexts for a composition in precisely drawn arabesques, with a dazzling polyphony of pure color . . ."[4] The artist himself accepts no more specific reading than that.

The hypothesis that the unifying link in the motifs is the bullfight[5] is, however, an attractive one. Aside from the bull, whose front-view eyes (and rear-view tail and genitals) are superimposed on his profile silhouette, there are three other motifs. Two, which frame the scene, are clearly human figures. The third, between the bull and the figure on the left, is a configuration that may or may not be a head.[6] Interpreted in terms of the bullfight hypothesis, the figure on the right, whose left hand holds a *muleta*, becomes a matador. The figure on the left becomes a *banderillero*—a surmise supported by his running posture, his raised arms, and by the tassled sombrero he wears in the preparatory sketch (fig. 62). The "head" between the *banderillero* and the bull can be read as a rear view of the picador's horse, the configurations of whose tail and sex echo the same motifs in the bull. His protective coat is indicated by the black band that parallels the lower edge of the picture field.

If indeed the bullfight played any role, even subconsciously, in Miró's choice of motifs for this picture, it would have been in keeping with an instinct to give such a large work a theme of ritual and collective character and importance. As demonstrated by *Guernica*, the *corrida* can function as a viable mythological substitute for the religious themes of older wall paintings, whose monumental size was sustained by subjects which, unlike those of modern painting in general, touched the common beliefs of the society.

XXIII *from* Barcelona Series. *1944. Lithograph, 24⅜ x 18⁹⁄₁₆ inches. (C&N, p. 132)*

XLVII *from* Barcelona Series. *1944. Lithograph, 10 x 13 inches. (C&N, p. 132)*

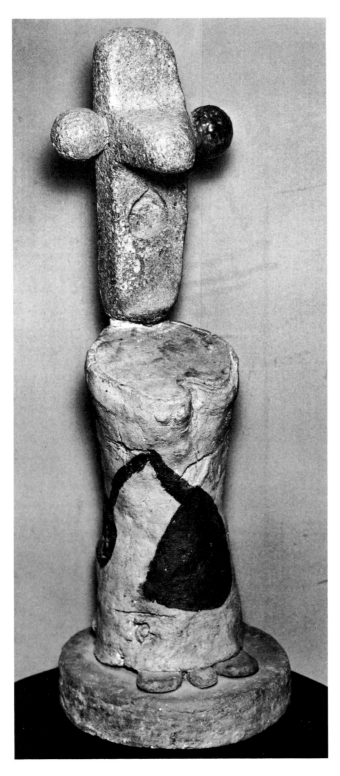

PERSONAGE. *Barcelona, 1947. Ceramic, 32½ inches high.* (C&N, p. 132)

HEAD. *Gallifa, 1954. Ceramic, 9½ x 18 inches.* (C&N, p. 132)

Miró began to work with the ceramist Lloréns Artigas in 1944. The two men had been friends since 1912, when Miró was an art student in Barcelona, and by the time of their more important collaborations in the later forties had developed the intuitive sense of shared creation that characterized artisanal workshops of earlier epochs. Their first efforts were simply ceramic plaques and vases on which Miró painted his familiar figures. In these the form belonged to Artigas, the surface design to Miró. Gradually, however, Miró became secure enough in the medium to attempt actual sculptures. He began by making models for these out of found materials, both natural and manmade (including bits of older sculptures). In 1953 Artigas's son Joan took over the task of translating these sculptures into clay forms, which Miró touched up when he thought editing necessary.

These two pieces are interesting as reflecting the special inflection Miró's language took on under the influence of ceramics. The body of the female *Personage* appears to have been developed from a section of tree trunk, the bark of the tree serving as a "costume," on which Miró painted with glazes. The association of the female "earth-mother" with a tree trunk is an idea that Miró had already given brilliant definition in a different form in the famous *Object of Sunset* (fig. 61), where the female sex symbol was painted on a tree-stump torso. The head of *Personage* is quite different in its totemic symmetry from the heads we see in Miró's paintings. There is something awesome and haunting about this eyeless face, to which two spheres are attached as ears, and whose mouth is essentially a negative of the spheres. Miró was obviously very pleased by this head. In fact, he remarked to its present owner that it was the first successful sculptural ceramic to emerge from his collaboration with Artigas. Twenty-three years later he enlarged it monumentally in *Tête de femme* (fig. 64).

Head shows another side of Miró's mastery of ceramics, one in which the supersubtle blending of tonalities in the glazes comes much more into play. The extraordinarily evocative outer contour and concave interior suggest an origin in a giant seashell, an association reinforced by the nacreous brilliance of the glazes. At the same time there is

something of an allusion to a skull, a poetic overtone strengthened in its turn by holes in the surface that represent the eyeballs and by the crackled white enamels of the outer contour. The nose is a beautiful piece of Miróesque improvisation, the nostrils forming, in their turn, the eyes of a skull-like head of a little personage whose legs wind around to suggest the cheekbones of the head of which it is a part. Miró also seems particularly attached to this conception and used a variant of *Head* as the upper part of his *Female Torso* of 1967 (fig. 65).

CONCRETE WRITING (Graphisme concret). *1953. Charcoal, brush, and ink, 19⅜ x 25⅛ inches. (C&N, p. 133)*

PERSON, WOMAN, BIRD, STAR AT SUNSET. *1953. Oil and gesso on gouged and burnt composition board, 42½ x 21½ inches. (C&N, p. 133)*

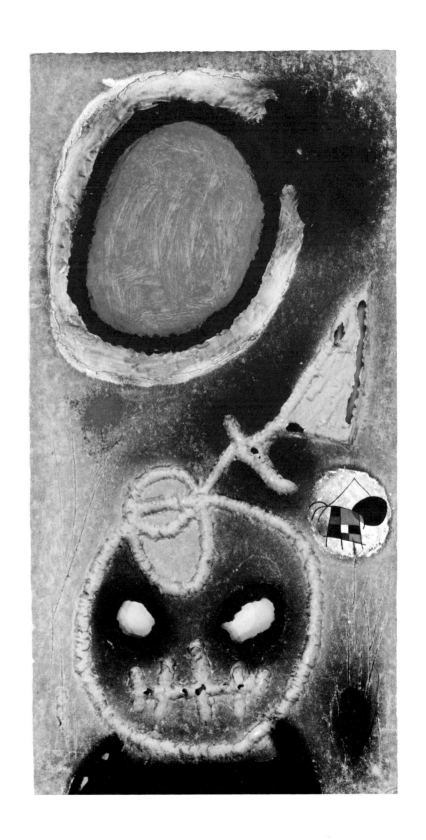

SERIES I, PLATE IV (The Family). *1952. Etching, engraving, and aquatint, printed in color, 14¹⁵⁄₁₆ x 17⅞ inches. (C&N, p. 133)*

EQUINOX. *1968. Etching and aquatint, printed in color,*
41¹⁄₁₆ x 29 inches. (C&N, p. 133)

THE SONG OF THE VOWELS. *Palma, April 1966. Oil on canvas, 12 feet 1/8 inch x 45 1/4 inches. (C&N, p. 133)*

The Song of the Vowels is one of Miró's most extraordinary paintings; even to those familiar with his œuvre it appears somewhat apart from the main body of his work. Yet its antecedents reach back into Miró's painting of the twenties. The idea of isolating disks and lozenges of pure color against a black ground was first explored in miniature scale in a drapery detail of *Dutch Interior* (p. 42); the combining of these forms, along with lines, in an allover pattern had closer precedents in the configurations of the Constellations (p. 81). Miró brought these pictorial ideas together in a group of six small pictures which immediately precede *The Song of the Vowels*, but which give no hint of its sweep and grandeur—nor of the transparency of its surface and ease of execution.

Unlike the Constellations, *The Song of the Vowels* has no personages, reveals no anecdotal scene. Its lyricism is more abstract—as if Miró, who was much involved with music in the Constellations, had sought a visual notation that might bring him closer to that art. Indeed, the very high, narrow, vertical format—unique in Miró's œuvre—is inherently abstract insofar as it automatically militates against the idea of landscape or the unfolding of narrative. (Horizontal formats of the same dimensions, which do tend to imply landscape or narrative, *are* occasionally found in Miró's work.) The unusual height of *The Song of the Vowels* immediately suggests a subject grander than human scale; Miró uses it to create a rainfall of color.

The "music" of *The Song of the Vowels*, the title suggests, refers to one of Miró's favorite poets, Rimbaud, who in "Voyelles" associated a particular color to each vowel. In the middle twenties, when Miró's art was more clearly referential and more directly influenced by poetry, he actually included the vowels in his imagery (fig. 66). Here he deals directly with the colors—although not just those identified by Rimbaud—and structures them in a hierarchy of sizes that suggest the range from a whole note to a hemidemisemiquaver, while distributing them in complex rhythms resembling musical subgroupings such as doublets and triplets.

But for all its musical abstractness, Miró's picture is still a far cry from the kind of post–World War II picture it superficially resembles.[1] There is always hovering about it the poetic suggestion of something other than just forms and colors. Rimbaud, after identifying a color with each vowel, went on to associate to it a whole universe of concrete images. Miró is less explicit. His disks and lines are suns, moons, and shooting stars by implication only—and through our familiarity with the prior appearances of these forms.

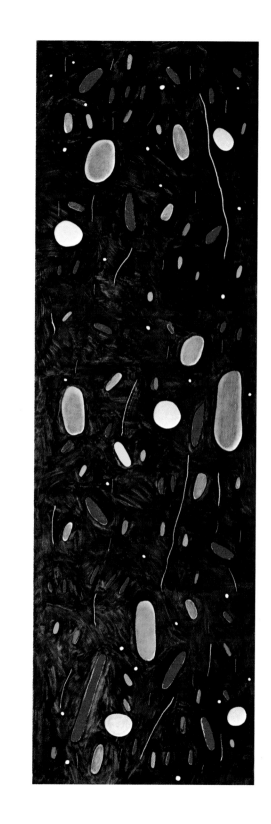

MOONBIRD. *1966. Bronze, 7 feet 8⅛ inches x 6 feet 9¼ inches x 59⅛ inches. (C&N, p. 134)*

Although from the late twenties onward Miró had executed a number of reliefs and constructions, he began to explore the possibilities of sculpture in the round only in the middle forties. Nevertheless, he traces his interest in the medium to his studies at the age of nineteen with Francisco Galí at the School of Fine Arts in Barcelona. "Galí was a remarkable teacher," Miró recalled, "and he gave me an exercise so that I would learn to 'see' form: He blindfolded me, and placed objects in my hands, and then asked me to draw the objects without having seen them . . . my interest in sculpture dates from that time—an interest that was renewed when I made ceramics with Artigas. Making sculpture is a very exciting experience for me—one in which I have become involved more and more."[1]

It was, to be sure, in 1944, the same year in which he began to collaborate with Artigas on ceramic sculpture, that Miró executed the foot-high bronze *Bird* (fig. 67) from which *Moonbird* grew twenty-two years later.[2] Although the latter is something more than a mere "pointing-up"[3] of the earlier work—Miró worked over the surfaces of the plaster for *Moonbird*—the changes are so slight that the 1944 bronze must be considered the first version or model of the Museum's sculpture.

The viewer who has only the weightless, volatile birds of Miró's painting in mind may at first find this bulky and monumental bronze—so resolutely anchored to the earth—a startling conception. Indeed, while *Moonbird* shares the morphology of Miró's painting, its ancestors are less to be found there than in the fertility idols of ancient and prehistoric peoples. It is less that *Moonbird* resembles such fetish sculptures than that it exhibits the same symmetry and ritual frontality. And its metamorphic ambiguities recall their syncretism. The crescent on the head, for example, is both a moon and a set of horns. This makes the bird secondarily a bull. This bird-bull is, however, also humanoid, since it stands on two powerful legs and its "wings" resemble arms.

Both birds and bulls are traditionally associated with sexuality, especially on the mythic and poetic level that *Moonbird* proclaims. This reference to procreation in the iconography is sustained in the contouring of *Moonbird*, which is a litany of forms that project outward, curve upward; even the eyeballs are phallic in this sense. The aggressive character of the sculpture is evident, and has

evoked vivid description: "Arrogant and hostile, this is a bird that would throw a stone at a personage. It is cocky, bullying, tumescent, all rampant libido."[4] Indeed, while sexuality in Miró is frequently only playful and gay,[5] it is raised here to a level of overwhelming power—but also of stability and order—as befits the cult symbol or totem of *miromonde*.

PERSONAGE AND BIRD. *Palma, 1968. Bronze, 41 x 25¼ x 7⅛ inches. (C&N, p. 135)*

Whereas *Moonbird* and other of Miró's sculptures derive from a tradition of modeling that goes back to ancient times, *Personage and Bird* belongs to a strictly modern conception of sculpture-making in which the work is assembled rather than modeled or carved. This procedure, which had earlier been used by both Picasso and Ernst among others, permits the incorporation of real objects into the work, as well as their translation into other entities within the iconographic context of the work itself. It may thus be seen as a three-dimensional extension of collage. The method is direct: "I don't begin the sculptures from drawings, but directly from the objects," Miró has said. ". . . I just put the objects together."[1]

Metamorphosis has been an abiding aspect of Miró's work since the middle twenties. But normally we see only the end result of the process. It is often Miró's pleasure to arrest the sculptural process at a point where the real objects he has appropriated are still identifiable as autonomous entities. In the case of certain of the polychrome assemblages of 1967, where the objects were painted individual colors,[2] the unity of the work suffered. *Personage and Bird* belongs to the following series, in which the surface of the bronze itself unifies the work. The head of the personage, for example, has clearly been cast from a wicker shopping basket pressed flat, its handles serving as ears; but even as the origin of this form is recognized, the eye generalizes it with the torso of the personage because of the common denominator of the "patina."

Actually *Personage and Bird* has no patina. Its markings are simply those with which it came out of the mold, as is the case with all the Miró sculptures cast at the Parellada foundry in Barcelona. Miró works with three foundries—Parellada, Susse, and Clementi (the latter two in the suburbs of Paris)—each of which has its own style and finish, and to which he confides each work according to its character. Susse, which specializes in giving works a classical patina, executed *Moonbird*. In the case of *Personage and Bird*, Miró chose Parellada so that the bronze surface would be preserved "in all its pristine wildness and power." The pieces he sends Parellada, "imagined in any other form," he maintains, "would be a dead loss."[3]

WOMAN WITH THREE HAIRS SURROUNDED BY BIRDS IN THE NIGHT. *Palma, September 1972. Oil on canvas, 95⅞ x 66½ inches. (C&N, p. 135)*

Miró is one of those artists who, like Matisse and Bonnard, maintain a single style or idiom throughout their maturity as painters. The conviction with which they assert their stylistic identity in the face of a fickle avant-garde whose goals turn alien, even hostile, is the measure of their authenticity. The vocabulary of such "single-vision" painters does not, however, go wholly unaltered. Beginning in the early forties, both Bonnard and Matisse moved toward simpler and more abstract definitions within their respective idioms—an economy made possible precisely through the distillation of a lifetime of exploring the same language. However inner-directed these mutations appear when viewed within these artists' œuvres, we are struck in retrospect by the way they parallel the broader change of taste within post–World War II painting.

Such is also the case with Miró. In its morphology and iconography, *Woman with Three Hairs Surrounded by Birds in the Night* can be regarded as of a piece with Miró's *personnages* of the mid-twenties and thirties. The woman's antennaelike hairs, the star, and the birds—in the simple arrow form of the one above her head or the more complex one to the right—are familiar configurations. Yet, juxtaposing this picture with Miró's works of earlier decades reveals more than just the way in which the principle of economy has operated within his style; also apparent is a relationship between this later work and a type of abstract painting common in Europe and America since 1950.

The most immediately recognizable difference between *Woman with Three Hairs* and its earlier prototypes in Miró is its total suppression of sculptural effects. Even the flattest of Miró's earlier pictures usually contained a few small modeled forms that served as contrasting accents. While the blue and green of this picture are shaded—thus setting off the opacity and evenness of the other colors— modeling itself is rigorously eschewed. Equally avoided (the ground is unpainted) is the undefined atmospheric space so common in Miró's earlier work. It is as if Miró's instincts toward three-dimensionality had been absorbed in his pursuit of sculpture. But while devoid of sculptural illusion, *Woman with Three Hairs* is invested with precisely that monumentality characteristic of Miró's major sculptures (p. 99). This is achieved by setting the large and simplified forms of the figure's silhouette so that they fill the space of the canvas almost to crowding.

Woman with Three Hairs derives from a palette (obtaining throughout Miró's work of recent years) reduced to the three primary and three secondary colors (of which the violet, rare in general in Miró's painting, is not present here at all). These colors, now standardized in his work, are never mixed or varied even slightly in hue, although they may vary in opacity, depending on their application. The picture began as a charcoal drawing on canvas in which the black areas alone were indicated. These areas (but not the contour lines) were painted in first; Miró says that this "always serves to give the composition equilibrium." The red was next; at the end of the session in which it was applied Miró put in just one spot of blue. "Then I studied the painting for a time before resuming," he recounts. "When all the red is in, I begin to know where to put the blue." The same procedure was repeated for the green, the lemon yellow, and the orange, in that order, in separate sessions sometimes weeks apart.

The ornamental skirt—and also the absorption of the woman's arms into the silhouette of her bust—is reminiscent of "The Matron," one of the most common figures in the typology of Majorcan folk sculpture (fig. 70). While direct citations of this art (of which Miró owns some excellent examples) are rare,[1] its presence has been strongly felt in his art, especially during the seventeen years that he has been living in Palma. Nor is it surprising that the particular reds, greens, blues, and yellows of this native art, set off always—as in this painting—against a white ground, should be extremely close to those which Miró has now standardized as his palette.

SOBRETEIXIM 5. *Palma, May 1972. Painted rope, wool, and wire mesh on hemp woven ground, 64 x 68 inches. (C&N, p. 135)*

Although Miró refers to the wall-hangings, his most recent foray into the exploitation of materials, as "tapestries," they have nothing in common with the actual tapestries that he has from time to time designed. Rather they represent an extension of collage, continuing an evolution the artist initiated in that medium in the late twenties. The generic title *Sobreteixim* is an old Catalan word referring to a decorative handwork in which varicolored patches of cloth were sewn onto a larger piece.

The woven grounds of the new works are executed in the workshop of Josep Royo according to indications by Miró. Like the rough grounds of certain collages (see p. 66) and the prepared grounds of many of the paintings, these serve primarily to stimulate pictorial ideas—such as the collaging, in *Sobreteixim 5*, of the heavy rope, whose broad strands are implied by the center section of the woven ground. In *Rope and People* (p. 69) the "otherness" of the rope in relation to the cardboard ground and the painted personages intensified its literal interpretation as something binding and torturing the figures; here the rope seems simply a material extension of the woven ground, just as the red and yellow yarn is a further development within the same family of materials. As there is no anecdotal reading, the unity of *Sobreteixim 5* is abstract, achieved through the interaction of its component parts.

The excitement of the work comes from the play of certain elements of Miró's basic vocabulary as they pass from one material to another. Thus the handsome "drawing" of the rope is answered by the heavily drawn black line in the upper left. The relation of that line to a patch of green which it contains is then echoed in the rope's relation to the red yarn and in the manner in which the purple is "enclosed" by the white disk.

The rawness of *Sobreteixim 5* reflects the artist's desire for immediacy. Miró seems to want to shortcut his familiar painterly materials, thus avoiding the habits of the hand and working with greater rapidity. The work has the air of being rapidly put together—as if profiting from a moment of intense inspiration.

CATALOG AND NOTES

WORKS ARE LISTED in the catalog in the order in which they appear in the body of the book. A date is enclosed in parentheses when it does not appear on the work. Dimensions are given in feet and inches, height preceding width; a third dimension, depth, is given for some sculptures. The author's last name alone is used in references to the following sources:

Dupin, Jacques, *Joan Miró: Life and Work* (New York: Harry N. Abrams, 1962).

Soby, James Thrall, *Joan Miró* (New York: The Museum of Modern Art, 1959).

TABLE WITH GLOVE
Paris, (winter) 1921
Oil on canvas, 46 x 35¼ inches
Signed lower left: "Miro / 1921"; and inscribed on stretcher: "Miró Nature Morte—Le gant et le Journal"
Provenance: Galerie Pierre, Paris; Pierre Matisse Gallery, New York; Sidney Janis Gallery, New York; The Donor, New York
Gift of Armand G. Erpf, 1955
Acq. no. 18.55
Ill. p. 17

1. The locations of Miró's studios in Paris are important, since they help date his contacts with other artists and writers. But the issue is complicated by contradictory testimony. Here is a brief review: In March 1919 Miró went to Paris for the first time and stayed in a hotel on the Rue Notre Dame des Victoires until June, when he returned to Montroig for the summer. The following winter he again went to Paris and, unable to find a studio, took a room in a hotel on the Boulevard Pasteur. It was not until after his return from Spain in late 1920 that he finally found a studio when the sculptor Pablo Gargallo, who had to leave Paris every winter to teach in Barcelona, let him have his at 45 Rue Blomet.

André Masson had the adjoining studio, and it was through Masson that Miró met Michel Leiris, Georges Limbour, Robert Desnos, and Antonin Artaud and became a part of the nucleus of what was to be the Surrealist group. It is difficult, however, to place the exact time of Miró's meeting with Masson. Miró himself says, "On my arrival in Paris in March 1919, I stopped at the Hôtel de la Victoire, Rue Notre Dame des Victoires. I stayed in Paris all the winter. That summer I went back to Spain, to the country. The next winter I am back again in Paris. I stopped at another hotel, number 32 Boulevard Pasteur. It is there that I had a visit from Paul Rosenberg. Picasso and Maurice Raynal had spoken to him about me. Sometime later Pablo Gargallo, who was spending the winter in Barcelona teaching sculpture at the Beaux Arts School, turned his studio over to me. It was at 45 Rue Blomet, next door to the Bal Nègre, still unknown to Parisians at that time as it had not yet been discovered by Robert Desnos. André Masson had the studio alongside. Only a partition separated us. In the Rue Blomet I began to work. I painted the *Tête d'une danseuse espagnole* which now belongs to Picasso, the *Table au gant*,

1. *The Table*, 1920. Gustav Zumsteg, Zurich

2. *Standing Nude*, 1921. Alsdorf Foundation, Chicago

109

3. *The Farm*, 1921–22. Mrs. Ernest Hemingway

4. *Grill and Carbide Lamp*, now lost, 1922–23

5. *The Tilled Field*, 1923–24. The Solomon R. Guggenheim Museum, New York

etc. . . . The next year it was not possible to get Gargallo's studio . . ." ("I Dream of a Large Studio," *XXe Siècle* [Paris], vol. 1, no. 2 [May–June 1938], pp. 25–28, translated by James Johnson Sweeney and published in *Joan Miró*, Pierre Matisse Gallery, New York, March 1940). This indicates Miró's first stay in Gargallo's studio was the winter of 1920–21.

The issue is further complicated elsewhere when Miró is quoted by James Johnson Sweeney, "Joan Miró: Comment and Interview," *Partisan Review* (New York), vol. xv, no. 2 (February 1948), p. 209: "At the time I was painting *The Farm* [1921–22], my first year in Paris, I had Gargallo's studio. Masson was in the studio next door." Masson recalls: "But Max Jacob had a salon! This salon was—La Savoyarde . . . And there, one day, I met Joan Miró, Joan Miró as unknown as myself. You can imagine; this was in 1922, '22, yes, in 1922, or maybe early '23; makes no difference. Miró said he was a painter. I told him I was too. I told him I was going to leave Montmartre because I had just rented a studio, at 45 Rue Blomet. He answered, 'It's curious, but I just rented a studio at the same place myself, a couple of days ago.'" This version, recorded in *André Masson: Entretiens avec Georges Charbonnier* (Paris: Julliard, 1958), p. 71, is unlikely, as we know that the winter of 1922–23 was the only winter until late 1927 that Miró did not spend in Gargallo's flat in the Rue Blomet. During that season of 1922–23 Artigas took Gargallo's studio and Miró stayed successively in a hotel on the Boulevard Raspail, a boardinghouse in the Rue Berthollet and later in Dubuffet's flat in the Rue Gay-Lussac. Most writers, including the author, have put the meeting between Masson and Miró in the winter of 1922–23. Assuming this to be inaccurate on the basis of Miró's absence from the Rue Blomet that winter, and considering the fallibility of the artists' memories after so many years, the most likely date for the meeting may be the winter of 1921–22, when Miró was finishing *The Farm*. Certainly Miró occupied Gargallo's studio in the Rue Blomet every winter, with the above exception, from the winter of 1920–21 until 1927, when he moved to a studio on the Rue Tourlaque, Cité des Fusains, in Montmartre.

2. Recounted to the author, summer 1972. (All subsequent direct or indirect quotations from Miró for which no source is given are from discussions between the artist and the author during the preparation of this book.)

3. Cf. *Horse, Pipe and Red Flower*, 1920 (Dupin, no. 70), and *The Table*, 1920 (fig. 1 and Dupin, no. 71).

THE CARBIDE LAMP
Montroig, Paris, 1922–23
Oil on canvas, 15 x 18 inches
Signed lower left: "Miró / 1922/23"; and lower right: "Miró / 1922–23"; inscribed on reverse: "Joan Miró / Nature Morte II / 1922–23"
Provenance: Pierre Loeb, Paris
Purchase, 1939
Acq. no. 12.39
Ill. p. 18

THE EAR OF GRAIN
Montroig, Paris, 1922–23
Oil on canvas, 14⅞ x 18⅛ inches
Signed lower left: "Miró / 1922–23"
Provenance: Pierre Loeb, Paris
Purchase, 1939
Acq. no. 11.39
Ill. p. 19

1. Montroig (Red Mountain), so called for the great purplish-red sandstone outcroppings that rise above it, lies about twenty-five miles south of Tarragona and is built on the slopes of foothills overlooking the coastal plain. The Miró farm acquired by the artist's father in 1910 is situated between the town and the sea and is but a short distance from the old town of Cornudella, familiar to Miró from his infancy as the home of his paternal grandfather, a blacksmith whose name was also Joan Miró.

2. J.-F. Rafols, in "Miró antes de la Masia," *Anales y Boletin de los Museos de Arte de Barcelona*, 1948, p. 497 ff., first used the term "detallista" to describe certain of Miró's works from the summer of 1918 through 1922, when he completed *The Farm*. The word has been adopted by Dupin (in its French form, "détailliste") and subsequent writers, who have also applied it to the prolix compositions of Miró's mature work.

3. Roland Tual was a poet and writer. One of the original members of the "Rue Blomet" group which included Leiris, Limbour, Artaud, and Salacrou, he was also the founder of the Galerie Surréaliste.

4. The reference here is to *Grill and Carbide Lamp* (fig. 4), now lost, not to the Museum's picture, *The Carbide Lamp*, in which an iron stand, not a grill, is represented.

5. Letter dated July 31, 1922. This excerpt is published for the first time, with the permission of Joan Miró and through the courtesy of Christian Tual, the recipient's son, Professor of English Literature at the Sorbonne.

6. According to Miró, Picasso said of this picture, on seeing it shortly after its completion, "C'est de la poésie."

7. See page 109, note 1.

THE HUNTER (CATALAN LANDSCAPE)
Montroig, Paris, 1923–24
Oil on canvas, 25½ x 39½ inches
Signed lower left: "Miró 1923–24"; and inscribed on reverse: "Joan Miró / Paysage Catalan / 1923–24"
Provenance: André Breton, Paris; Mme Simone Collinet, Paris
Purchase, 1936
Acq. no. 95.36
Ill. p. 23

1. Shown for the first time in a one-man exhibition at the Galerie Pierre, Paris, June 12–27, 1925, as "Le Chasseur," this painting is inscribed on the reverse "Paysage catalan" (no longer visible because of lining) and has often been exhibited and referred to as "Catalan Landscape." At Miró's request the painting is now titled as it was in its initial showing, with the inscribed title following in parentheses.

2. Although the sense of crisis Miró felt in 1937 in personal terms and in regard to the war in Spain was to cause him to return to a kind of realism in a series of drawings done from life at the Académie de la Grande Chaumière, in *Still Life with Old Shoe* (p. 73), and in *Self-Portrait I* (p. 77), these works, as Jacques Dupin observes (p. 296), were "no more than a means for surmounting the depression and anguish that were paralyzing him. Reality is at this time merely a refuge and a support . . ." The later "realistic" works were permeated by a visionary, almost apocalyptic character wholly at odds with the realism of his pre-1923 work and continuous in spirit with the works that surround them.

3. See Dupin, pp. 96, 98; Roland Penrose, *Miró* (New York: Harry N. Abrams, 1969), pp. 12–13, 32–33.

4. Dupin, p. 139.

5. Letter to Ricart, July 1920, cited in Dupin, p. 98.

6. Letter, late summer 1923, cited in Dupin, p. 139.

7. For Miró and biomorphism see the author's *Dada and Surrealist Art* (New York: Harry N. Abrams, 1969), p. 19 and pp. 152–56.

8. Rosalind Krauss and Margit Rowell in *Magnetic Fields* (New York: Solomon R. Guggenheim Foundation, 1972), p. 74, identify the lizard as "Merlin the wizard, fitted with his traditional conic hat," from Guillaume Apollinaire's *L'Enchanteur pourrissant*.

9. The dissociation of ideas and their subsequent reordering is basic to the collage technique and, as such, became a tool in the plastic expression of Surrealist theory. See the author's *Dada and Surrealist Art*, pp. 116, 121–22.

10. For a definition of peinture-poésie in the context of Surrealism, see the author's *Dada, Surrealism, and Their Heritage* (New York: The Museum of Modern Art, 1968), p. 64.

11. Most of the identifications of objects in the iconographic chart were indicated by Miró on a visit to the Museum in 1959; the identifications were recently supplemented by Miró in conversations with the author.

12. R. T. Doepel, *Aspects of Joan Miró's Stylistic Development, 1920–1925*, unpublished M.A. thesis, Courtauld Institute, University of London, 1967.

13. Actually Miró's expression, which the author was not able to note verbatim on this occasion, suggested fervency tinged by the romantic and the passionate, close to the archaic *feux ardents*.

6. *Vines and Olive Trees*, 1919. Mr. and Mrs. Leigh B. Block, Chicago

7. Fragment from the apse of Sant Climent de Taull, Lérida, Spain, A.D. 1123. Museo de Arte de Cataluña, Barcelona

8. Redon, *The Eye Like a Strange Balloon Mounts toward Infinity*, 1882. The Museum of Modern Art, New York

14. This creature has erroneously been interpreted as "a dead bird" (Penrose, p. 38) and a "leashed dog" (Soby, p. 37, quoting Alfred H. Barr, Jr., in *Masters of Modern Art* [New York: The Museum of Modern Art, 1954], p. 142).

15. For discussion see Krauss and Rowell, pp. 77–78.

16. Ibid., p. 77.

17. Gerta Moray, "Miró, Bosch and Fantasy Painting," *The Burlington Magazine* (London), vol. CXIII, no. 820 (July 1971), p. 387, proposes paintings by Bosch as the source of this and other motifs in Miró's painting of 1923–25. Miró himself has said that these were not sources for him, at least insofar as he was aware; but he does note that Bosch has always been one of his favorite painters. It is certainly possible that subconscious recollections of the latter's pictures are reflected in *The Hunter*. As there were equally immediate sources for these motifs in Romanesque art, and more immediate ones in modern art, it is certain that Moray has overestimated Bosch as a source. Indeed, she has entirely misread certain motifs in the painting in order to confirm her thesis.

18. For example, *The Eye Like a Strange Balloon Mounts toward Infinity* (fig. 8). Masson was a great admirer of Redon and frequently brought his work to Miró's attention.

19. See Krauss and Rowell, p. 77, who single out in particular a collage (fig. 9) from Ernst's *Repetitions* (1922) showing a string pulled through the eye parallel to the lower edge of the picture, thus suggesting Miró's horizon line.

20. Dupin (p. 140) interprets the following quotation from a Miró letter to Rafols as referring only to *The Hunter:* "Hard at work and full of enthusiasm. Monstrous animals and angelic animals. *Trees with ears and eyes and a peasant in a Catalan cap*, holding a shotgun and smoking a pipe" (italics mine). In fact, as Miró has told the author, he was referring to two pictures, *The Tilled Field*, which does depict a tree with both an ear and an eye, and *The Hunter*, in which the peasant is presented as described. The tree with the eye, referred to in Miró's letter, is a reference to *The Tilled Field*. He does not consider the conjunction of the eye and the carob tree as meaning that the former is growing out of the latter as it does in the earlier picture.

21. Despite the fact that it is black, there is no doubt that this shape is the sun, as Miró has so identified it in conversation with the author and in the iconographic chart. (Cf. Moray, pp. 387, 388, 391, where the writer speaks of a "puzzling Miró motif," that is, "a black sacred heart in the sky," and observes that "The Sacred Heart, which Miró has shown in place of the sun, is depicted in black, the colour of death.")

22. *See* "The Harlequin's Carnival," text reproduced in the author's *Dada and Surrealist Art*, p. 154. This observation is to be found in Krauss and Rowell, p. 78.

23. Notably, *The Somersault*, 1924 (fig. 11), and *Landscape with Rooster*, 1927 (fig. 12).

24. A sketch for the painting *Novia* (the full title in English is "Sweetheart of the First Occupant") served as the cover of the first issue of *391* (January 25, 1917), a review whose first four numbers were published by Picabia in collaboration with Albert Gleizes, Marie Laurencin, and Max Goth in Barcelona. It was at this time, at the dealer Dalmau's, that Miró met Picabia.

25. Although Moray (p. 387) suggests that the wheel motif may have been derived from Bosch, Miró, as has been observed, questions this (see note 17). There seems no doubt that the machine image, in particular the wheel, came primarily through Picabia, with whose work Miró had long been familiar.

26. Beyond Miró's personal history, there is, of course, a long-standing affinity between the cultures of Catalonia and France that derives from their common border and once-common language (Catalan, which is still in wide use—Miró speaks it, just as did Picasso—belongs to the Occitanian or Provençal family of tongues). From 795, when Charlemagne drove the Moors from Catalonia, until the eleventh century, the province was an integral part of France, actively sharing the Carolingian cultural and economic expansion. Formal ties with France were severed in 1258 with the Treaty of Corbeil signed by St. Louis. Although its subsequent history is entwined with that of Aragon, there exists to this day an independent "Catalanism" which may be said to lean toward France. In 1640, when the Spanish monarch Philip IV attempted to deprive Catalonia of its rights and privileges, it gave itself up to Louis XIII of France and was not restored to Spain until 1659. From 1808 to 1813 it was again held by France. In 1932 Catalonia organized itself as an autonomous republic and fought the Franco troops until the end of the Civil War (Barcelona did not fall until January 26, 1939).

27. Soby, p. 37. While pinks, yellows, and terra-cotta tones are found in Miró's earlier work, they lack the transparent character of the "al fresco" colors in the Romanesque frescoes of Catalonia. *The Hunter* is the first work in which Miró achieved with these colors the tonal transparency characteristic of the frescoes he so loves.

28. Beyond the carob tree, the only other particularized plant shown in *The Hunter* is the triangular grape vine, identified above (29) in a terrain manured by an animal turd (28). That Miró associates this perforated triangle with fertility is confirmed by its presence among a woman's pubic hairs in *Portrait of Madame K.* (fig. 18), begun shortly after *The Hunter*. Later, in a metaphoric extension of the idea of fertility, it would symbolize the painter's palette.

29. Soby (p. 37), quoting Alfred Barr, *Masters of Modern Art*, p. 142, and Penrose (p. 38), who leans toward calling this creature a rabbit, but because of its body shape and "triangular fish-like tail" settles on "ambiguous creature." Moray (p. 391), rejecting Dupin's assertion that the image is of a fish, wrongly insists that it "is in fact clearly a rabbit."

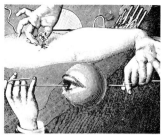

9. Ernst, *Collage*, 1922. Cover design for Paul Eluard, *Répétitions, Dessins de Max Ernst* (Paris: Au sans Pareil, 1922)

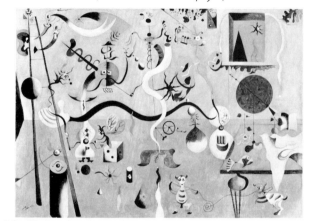

10. *The Harlequin's Carnival*, 1924–25. Albright-Knox Art Gallery, Buffalo, New York

11. *The Somersault*, 1924. Yale University Art Gallery, New Haven, Connecticut. Gift of Collection Société Anonyme

12. *Landscape with Rooster*, 1927. Private collection, New York

13. Picabia, *Novia*, 1917

14. *Automaton*, 1924. Mr. and Mrs. Morton G. Neumann, Chicago

30. Sweeney, *Joan Miró* (New York: The Museum of Modern Art, 1941), p. 28; Soby, p. 38. Dupin (pp. 141–42) recognizes the letters as standing for "sardine" but feels that this "unanimous interpretation [as the *sardana*] is perfectly in the spirit of Miró's mode of expression." The artist, however, insists that reference to the *sardana* is entirely misleading.

Moray (p. 391), although aware of Dupin's interpretation, nevertheless wrongly insists that the letters are "surely an amputation of the word *sardana*." In a footnote she proffers the interesting hypothesis that "it is tempting to regard the syllable *sard* as a deliberate pun in the manner of Picabia and Duchamp, since the word sardine is a colloquialism for phallus in Catalan." Since Miró rejects the idea that the letters were thus intended, the pun would have had to be an unconscious one.

31. Miró's and Masson's images of flames and the latter's title, *The Four Elements*, reflect the Surrealist interest in alchemy that was to become dominant in the Second Manifesto, in which Rimbaud, Poe, and Sade are rejected but fourteenth-century alchemists such as Nicolas Flamel are celebrated. About *The Four Elements* Masson has said: "What do these Four Elements represent? What they represent is this: I am paying tribute to elemental forces. Now this tribute to the elemental forces wasn't something exactly . . . let's see . . . on the beaten track of painting, you'll agree. After all, this picture has certain, let's say, metaphysical pretensions" (*Entretiens avec Georges Charbonnier*, p. 49). The Miró too is, in a sense, a celebration of the four elements in its fusion of earth, sea, and sky with the human, animal, and vegetable life that thrives upon them.

32. The dotted lines have been seen as relating to de Chirico (Krauss and Rowell, p. 78), but Miró rejects this thesis, observing that the dotted lines in de Chirico usually represent "seams," whereas he saw breaking up of the line simply as a means of "changing its speed." Doepel, *Aspects of Joan Miró's Stylistic Development, 1920–1925*, suggests that "the dotted line in the figure in the *Catalan Landscape* may be paralleled to the graphic convention used in making copies of cave paintings. Such lines indicate where an image has been reconstructed and is frequently found in reproductions in Spanish periodicals published in the second decade of the century." Barr, *Masters of Modern Art*, p. 142, describes the dotted line in *The Hunter* as "a trail that winds before him," a reading that is supported by the 1924 drawing, *Nude Descending a Staircase* (fig. 20). This drawing was called to my attention by my colleague Kynaston McShine.

15. Bosch, *The Haywain*. Museo Nacional del Prado, Madrid

18. *Portrait of Madame K.*, 1924. Mme Jeanne Gaffé, Cagnes-sur-Mer

16. *Dog Barking at the Moon*, 1926. Philadelphia Museum of Art, A. E. Gallatin Collection

19. Calder, *Lobster Trap and Fish Tail*, 1939. The Museum of Modern Art, New York

17. *The Deluge*, fol. 85 from the *Apocalypse of Saint-Sever*, 1028–72. Bibliothèque Nationale, Paris

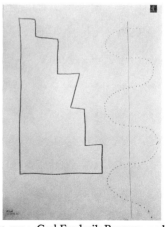

20. *Nude Descending a Staircase*, 1924. Carl Frederik Reutersward, Lausanne

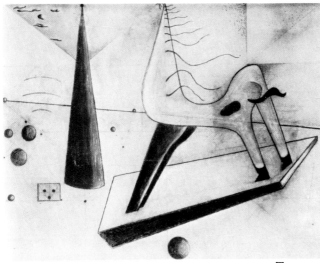

21. *Toys*, 1924

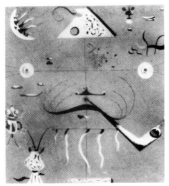

22. *Head of a Peasant*, 1924–25

23. *Head of a Catalan Peasant*, 1925.
Private collection, London

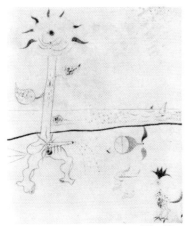

24. *The Trap*, 1924. Estate of André Breton

THE FAMILY

Paris, (early) 1924
Black and red chalk on emery paper, 29½ x 41 inches
Signed lower right: "Miró / 1924"
Provenance: René Gaffé, Brussels; Minneapolis Institute of
  Arts; The Donors, New York
Gift of Mr. and Mrs. Jan Mitchell, 1961
Acq. no. 395.61
Ill. p. 29

1. Dupin, p. 144.

2. See p. 21.

THE BIRTH OF THE WORLD

Montroig, (summer) 1925
Oil on canvas, 8 feet ½ inch x 6 feet 4¾ inches
Signed lower right: "Miró / 1925"; and on reverse:
  "Joan Miró / 1925"
Provenance: René Gaffé, Brussels and Cagnes-sur-Mer;
  Jeanne Gaffé, Cagnes-sur-Mer
Acquired through an anonymous fund, the Mr. and Mrs.
  Joseph Slifka and Armand G. Erpf Funds, and by gift from
  the artist, 1972
Acq. no. 262.72
Ill. p. 31

1. Dupin includes (pp. 157, 161) *The Birth of the World* in the series he designates "dream paintings," all of which, he states, were executed in Paris; Miró, however, distinctly recalls painting *The Birth of the World* in Montroig during the summer.

2. Gaffé in *A la verticale: Réflexions d'un collectionneur* (Brussels: André de Rache, 1963), p. 108, claims to have bought this picture "as soon as it was finished," but Miró has told the author that the painting was in his studio for "at least a year" after he had finished it. In the same passage as the quote above Gaffé mentions his astonishment at and admiration for the pictures hanging on Miró's studio walls at 22 Rue Tourlaque; the address given suggests that it may even have been 1927 when Gaffé bought *The Birth of the World*.

3. As recounted to the author in November 1967.

4. *Joan Miró*, Palais des Beaux Arts, Brussels, January 6–February 7, 1956, no. 15 in the catalog.

5. In an interview with the author, June 1959. Breton actually erred slightly in the title of the painting, but there is no question that he was referring to *The Birth of the World*.

6. *Le Surréalisme et la peinture* (New York and Paris: Brentano's, 1945, 2nd edition; originally published 1928 by Gallimard), p. 68.

7. Interview with the author, June 1959.

8. *Manifeste du surréalisme* (Paris: Editions du Sagittaire, 1924), p. 42.

9. Shortly after meeting André Breton in the winter of 1923–24 Masson began making his first automatic drawings, which preceded Miró's first excursions into automatism by over a year.

10. Conversation between Miró and Masson in 1924; recounted to the author by Masson, who has also told Dupin of the remark (Dupin, p. 142).

11. For discussion of the range of Surrealist styles, see the author's *Dada, Surrealism, and Their Heritage*, pp. 64–66.

12. *Entretiens 1913–1952* (Paris: Gallimard, 1952), p. 56.

13. Cited by Sweeney, "Joan Miró: Comment and Interview," p. 212.

14. Though in much smaller format, such microbiological images on a ground evoking stained litmus paper are to be found in the work of Klee, for example, in *Adam and Little Eve* (fig. 27). Miró was introduced to Klee through a book of reproductions lent to him by Masson; subsequently he saw his work in private collections and at the Galerie Vavin-Raspail, which held the first one-man show of his work in Paris, October 21–November 14, 1925. Both Klee and Miró, along with Arp, de Chirico, Ernst, Masson, Picasso, Man Ray, and Pierre Roy, were represented in the first group exhibition of Surrealist painting at the Galerie Pierre, Paris, November 14–25, 1925.

25. Matta, *The Earth Is a Man*, 1942. Mr. and Mrs. Joseph R. Shapiro, Oak Park, Illinois

26. Matta, *Le Vertige d'Eros*, 1944. The Museum of Modern Art, New York

27. Klee, *Adam and Little Eve*, 1921

28. *The Statue*, 1925. Marcel Mabille, Rhode St-Genèse, Belgium

29. Picasso, *Three Dancers*, 1925. The Tate Gallery, London

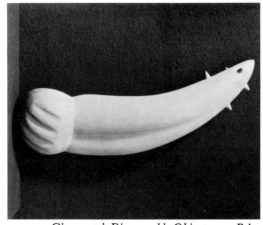

30. Giacometti, *Disagreeable Object*, 1931. Private collection, New York

31. *Cadavre exquis:* Tzara, Hugo, Knutsen, Breton, c. 1926. Mr. and Mrs. Morton G. Neumann, Chicago

THE STATUE
May 1926
Conté crayon on buff paper, 24½ x 18¾ inches
Signed lower right: "Miró / 5–26"
Provenance: Galerie Bonaparte, Paris
Purchase, 1936
Acq. no. 86.36
Ill. p. 34

1. The terminology used by Meyer Schapiro in his lectures at Columbia University. See also Schapiro cited in "A *Life* Round Table on Modern Art," *Life* (New York), vol. xxv, no. 15 (October 11, 1948), p. 59. In discussing the "internal image" of the body in his lectures, Schapiro refers frequently to Paul Schilder's *Image and Appearance of the Human Body*, Psyche Monograph No. 4 (London: George Routledge and Sons Ltd., 1935).

FIGURE (*cadavre exquis:* sections from top to bottom by Tanguy, Miró, Max Morise, and Man Ray)
1926 or 1927
Ink, pencil, color crayon, 14¼ x 9 inches
Reverse inscribed in each section in same hand: "Tanguy / Miró / Max Morise / 1926 or 27 / Man Ray"
Provenance: André Breton, Paris
Purchase, 1935
Acq. no. 260.35
Ill. p. 35

1. Observed by Margit Rowell in conversation with the author and discussed in her essay "Magnetic Fields: The Poetics" in Krauss and Rowell, *Magnetic Fields*, p. 41.

PERSON THROWING A STONE AT A BIRD
Montroig, (summer) 1926
Oil on canvas, 29 x 36¼ inches
Signed lower left: "Miró / 1926"
Provenance: René Gaffé, Brussels
Purchase, 1937
Acq. no. 271.37
Ill. p. 36

1. Among the thirteen other paintings in this series executed at Montroig in the summers of 1926 and 1927 are: *Hand Catching a Bird*, 1926 (Dupin, no. 174); *Dog Barking at the Moon*, 1926 (fig. 16 and Dupin, no. 177); *Landscape with Rooster*, 1927 (fig. 12 and Dupin, no. 181); and *Animated Landscape*, 1927 (Dupin, no. 182).

2. For discussion see the chapter "A Post-Cubist Morphology" in the author's *Dada and Surrealist Art*, pp. 18–22.

LANDSCAPE
Montroig, (summer) 1927
Oil on canvas, 51⅛ x 76⅜ inches
Signed lower left: "Miró / 1927"
Provenance: Pierre Colle, Paris; Pierre Matisse Gallery,
  New York
Promised gift of Mr. and Mrs. Gordon Bunshaft, New York
Ill. p. 39

1. First suggested by R. T. Doepel, *Aspects of Joan Miró's Stylistic Development.* For a further discussion see Krauss and
Rowell, *Magnetic Fields,* p. 114.

2. Krauss and Rowell, *Magnetic Fields,* ibid.

3. Ibid.

Colored postcard of Hendrick Maertensz Sorgh's
  THE LUTANIST, 1661; Rijksmuseum, Amsterdam
5½ x 3⅝ inches
Gift of Joan Miró, 1973
Ill. p. 40

STUDY FOR DUTCH INTERIOR I
Montroig, (summer 1928)
Pencil on graph paper, 3⅝ x 2¼ inches
Gift of the artist, 1973
Acq. no. 119.73
Ill. p. 40

STUDY FOR DUTCH INTERIOR I
Montroig, (summer 1928)
Pencil on graph paper, 3¼ x 2¼ inches
Gift of the artist, 1973
Acq. no. 120.73
Ill. p. 40

STUDY FOR DUTCH INTERIOR I
Montroig, (summer 1928)
Pencil, 6⅛ x 4⅝ inches
Gift of the artist, 1973
Acq. no. 121.73
Ill. p. 40

STUDY FOR DUTCH INTERIOR I
Montroig, (summer 1928)
Pencil, 6⅛ x 4⅝ inches
Gift of the artist, 1973
Acq. no. 122.73
Ill. p. 40

STUDY FOR DUTCH INTERIOR I
Montroig, (summer 1928)
Pencil and white chalk, 6 x 4¾ inches
Gift of the artist, 1973
Acq. no. 123.73
Ill. p. 41

STUDY FOR DUTCH INTERIOR I
Montroig, (summer 1928)
Pencil and pen and ink, 8⅝ x 6⅝ inches
Gift of the artist, 1973
Acq. no. 124.73
Ill. p. 41

STUDY FOR DUTCH INTERIOR I
Montroig, (summer 1928)
Pencil, 10½ x 8 inches
Gift of the artist, 1973
Acq. no. 125.73
Ill. p. 41

CARTOON FOR DUTCH INTERIOR I
Montroig, (summer 1928)
Charcoal and pencil, 24⅝ x 18⅝ inches
Ruled and numbered for transfer of composition to canvas
Gift of the artist, 1973
Acq. no. 126.73
Ill. p. 41, foldout

DUTCH INTERIOR I
Montroig, (summer) 1928
Oil on canvas, 36⅛ x 28¾ inches
Signed on reverse: "Joan Miró / 'Interieur Hollandais' / 1928"
Provenance: (Zwemmer Gallery, London); Galerie Pierre,
  Paris; Georges Keller, New York
Mrs. Simon Guggenheim Fund, 1945
Acq. no. 163.45
Ill. p. 42, foldout

1. The others in this series are: *Dutch Interior II* (Dupin, no.
235), Peggy Guggenheim Collection, Venice; *Dutch Interior
III* (fig. 32 and Dupin, no. 236), Mrs. Wolfgang Schoenborn
Collection, New York. Stylistically indistinguishable from the
three interiors, *The Potato* (Dupin, no. 237) might also be included in this group, as Dupin (pp. 189–92) points out.

2. First observed by Walter Erben, *Joan Miró* (New York:
George Braziller, 1959), p. 125. Miró recently donated to The
Museum of Modern Art the color postcard that he purchased
at the time of his 1928 trip to Holland, as well as the suite of
eight preparatory drawings (pp. 40–41) for the Museum's
painting that the card inspired.

3. Cf. Erben, p. 126.

4. Professor Colin Eisler of the Institute of Fine Arts, New
York University, has pointed out to the author that the painting on the wall in Sorgh's picture, according to a Rijksmuseum
catalog, actually depicts Thisbe discovering the body of Pyramus. In Miró's reading of the scene, the disguised Thisbe,
bending over the recumbent form, was mistaken for an as-
sailant.

5. Among examples of Miró's use of his handprint are: *Woman
Dreaming of Escape,* 1945 (Dupin, no. 653); *Woman in the*

32. *Dutch Interior III*, 1928. Mrs. Wolfgang Schoenborn, New York

33. *Collage*, 1929. P.-G. Bruguière, Paris

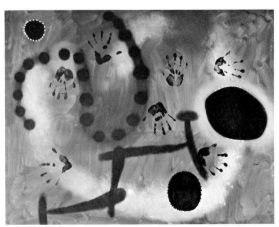

34. *Hope Comes Back to Us as the Constellations Flee*, 1954.
Galerie Maeght, Paris

Night, 1945 (Dupin, no. 654); *Hope Comes Back to Us as the Constellations Flee*, 1954 (fig. 34 and Dupin, no. 852). Miró may have been influenced by paleolithic cave paintings in this regard. See James Johnson Sweeney, "Miró," *Art News Annual* (New York), vol. XXIII, 1954, pp. 65, 69.

Photo of an engraving by T. R. Smith after George Engleheart's
  PORTRAIT OF MRS. MILLS
10¼ x 8⅛ inches
Gift of Joan Miró, 1973
Ill. p. 46

STUDY FOR PORTRAIT OF MISTRESS MILLS IN 1750
Paris, (early 1929)
Pencil on lined paper, 5¼ x 4¼ inches
Inscribed lower right center: "mon chéri"
Gift of the artist, 1973
Acq. no. 127.73
Ill. p. 46

STUDY FOR PORTRAIT OF MISTRESS MILLS IN 1750
Paris, (early 1929)
Pencil, 8½ x 6⅝ inches
Inscribed lower center: "'Portrait de femme' /
  'Portrait de Mme M (1890)'"
Gift of the artist, 1973
Acq. no. 128.73
Ill. p. 46

STUDY FOR PORTRAIT OF MISTRESS MILLS IN 1750
Paris, (early 1929)
Pencil, 8⅛ x 6⅝ inches
Inscribed (and crossed out) lower right: "my dear"
Gift of the artist, 1973
Acq. no. 129.73
Ill. p. 46

CARTOON FOR PORTRAIT OF MISTRESS MILLS IN 1750
Paris, (early 1929)
Charcoal and pencil, 24¾ x 19 inches
Ruled and numbered for transfer of composition to canvas
Gift of the artist, 1973
Acq. no. 130.73
Ill. p. 47

PORTRAIT OF MISTRESS MILLS IN 1750
Paris, (early) 1929
Oil on canvas, 45½ x 35 inches
Signed on reverse: "Joan Miró / 1929 / 'Portrait de Mistress
  Mills / en 1750'"
Provenance: Mrs. Valentine Dudensing, New York
Promised gift of James Thrall Soby, New Canaan,
  Connecticut
Ill. p. 48

1. Although shown and published under the title *Portrait of Mrs. Mills in 1750* until the late 1960s, the "Mrs." has been changed to "Mistress" to conform to the artist's inscription on the reverse of the canvas (see catalog entry).

2. Miró does not recall whether he worked originally from an engraving after Engleheart's painting or a reproduction of such an engraving; his then source has been lost, but he recalls that it was *not* a postcard or photograph of the painting itself. Miró has, however, given the Museum a recent photograph of the engraving along with preparatory drawings for this picture (pp. 46, 47).

3. Picasso's translations of older pictures begin with a series of variations executed in 1932 after the Crucifixion panel of Matthias Grünewald's Isenheim Altarpiece. See Christian Zervos, *Pablo Picasso*, 25 vols. published to date (Paris: Editions Cahiers d'Art, 1932–72), vol. VIII, nos. 49–56.

4. See Soby, p. 62.

5. When he gave these drawings to the author in January 1973 as a gift to The Museum of Modern Art, Miró numbered them. Since he numbered the photograph of the engraving after Engleheart number I, the first drawing was numbered II; this Miró identified as the one published here (p. 46) as 2 in a series which does not include the engraving. The author, after careful study, concluded that Miró was mistaken regarding the order. Moreover, the Miró marked as III, a drawing (fig. 35) on the reverse of the sheet he marked as IV, is not, the author believes, a part of the *Mistress Mills* series, but a study for Miró's *La Fornarina* (fig. 36) after a painting attributed to Raphael (fig. 37). As this drawing was on the verso of one in Miró's folder of studies for *Mistress Mills*, his error was a perfectly understandable one. For the record, the following are the two sequences of images as numbered by Miró and by the author.

35. *Study for La Fornarina (after Raphael)*, 1929. The Museum of Modern Art, New York

36. *La Fornarina (after Raphael)*, 1929. Galerie Maeght, Paris

37. Attributed to Raphael, *La Fornarina*. Galleria Nazionale d'Arte Antica, Palazzo Barberini, Rome

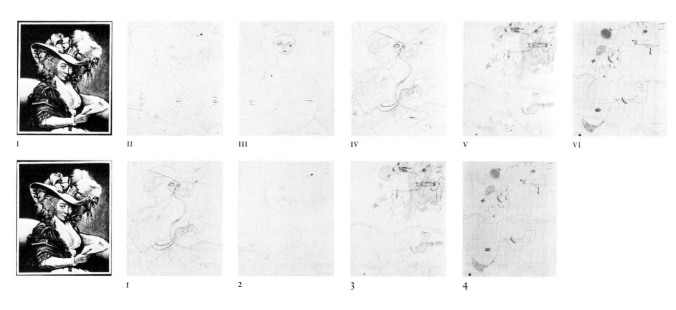

I   II   III   IV   V   VI

I   2   3   4

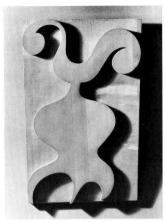

38. Arp, *Mme Torso with Wavy Hat*, 1916. Rupf-Stiftung, Kunstmuseum, Bern

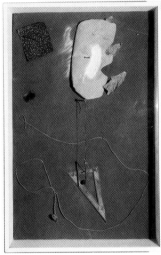

39. *Spanish Dancer*, 1928. Mr. and Mrs. Morton G. Neumann, Chicago

40. *Painting, 1930*. Menil Family Collection, Houston

6. In 1927 Miró moved from the Rue Blomet to a studio in Montmartre found for him by his dealer, Jacques Viot, on the Rue Tourlaque, where Max Ernst, René Magritte, Paul Eluard, and Jean Arp were already living. Miró kept this studio until after his marriage in October of 1929, when on returning to Paris with his bride he moved to a small apartment at 3 Rue François-Mouthon, and was, once again, without a studio.

7. First observed by Soby, p. 66.

8. More than any other major colorist after Bonnard and Matisse, Miró understood that density of *matière* not only failed to add to the effulgence of color, but indeed tended to diminish it, insofar as the eye perceived the tactility of the impasto and was forced to experience it simultaneously with the hue. See discussion p. 25.

9. Cited in Soby, pp. 26–28.

COLLAGE
Montroig, summer 1929
Pastel, ink, watercolor, crayon, and paper collage, 28⅝ x 42¾ inches
Signed on reverse: "Miró / Eté 1929"
Provenance: Galerie Lawrence, Paris; Robert Elkon Gallery, New York; Maurice Rheims and Victor Hammer, Paris; Crane Kalman Gallery, London
James Thrall Soby Fund, 1968
Acq. no. 1307.68
Ill. p. 51

1. Although the colored papers in this collage have faded, Miró, who examined it on a visit to the Museum in June 1968, declared that he liked it better for the patina of age. A work of art, he said at the time, should be "living and not embalmed."

2. On the occasion of the visit mentioned above, Miró said that the edges of the collage elements had always drawn away from the surface, that they were so intended, and that in no circumstance were they to be flattened.

3. See the author's *Dada and Surrealist Art*, p. 256.

RELIEF CONSTRUCTION
Montroig, (summer) 1930
Wood and metal, 35⅞ x 27⅝ inches
Signed on reverse: "Joan Miró / 1930"
Provenance: André Breton, Paris; Paul Eluard, Paris
Purchase, 1937
Acq. no. 259.37
Ill. p. 53

1. Penrose, in *Picasso: His Life and Work* (London: Victor Gollancz, 1958), p. 232, reports: "Another example of his [Picasso's] 'malicious art' is the large collage of the same year, 1926, called *Guitar*, in which the main element is a coarse dishcloth perforated by nails whose points stick out viciously from the picture. Picasso told me that he had thought of embedding razor blades in the edges of the picture so that whoever went

to lift it would cut their hands. There are no decorative curves to soften the cruel impact of the picture and there is no charm of colour. It is an aggressive and powerful expression of anger in a language which makes it painfully plain."

PERSONNAGE AU PARAPLUIE
Montroig, (summer 1931)
Wood furniture frames, dowel, umbrella, and artificial flowers, c. 6 feet high
Original (shown in photograph, p. 54) lost; replica constructed by artist, 1973
Gift of the artist, 1973
Ill. p. 54

1. Such speculations were prompted not unnaturally by Miró's own frequently expressed intense interest in Jarry's work, particularly *Le Surmâle*. In 1948, looking back over the years, Miró told James Johnson Sweeney ("Comment and Interview," p. 209): "The poets Masson introduced me to interested me more than the painters I had met in Paris. I was carried away by the new ideas they brought and especially the poetry they discussed. I gorged myself on it all night long—poetry principally in the tradition of Jarry's *Surmâle*." For further discussion see Rowell, "Magnetic Fields: The Poetics," Krauss and Rowell, p. 44.

2. In conjunction with the Miró retrospective to be held at the Grand Palais, Paris, in 1974, ballet performances with decor designed by Miró will be presented.

OBJECT
1931
Assemblage: painted wood, steel, string, bone, and a bead, 15¾ inches high, at base 8¼ x 4¾ inches
Signed under base: "Miró / 1931"
Provenance: Georges Hugnet, Paris; Richard Feigen Gallery, Chicago; Burt Kleiner, Los Angeles; Richard Feigen Gallery, Chicago; The Donors, Chicago
Gift of Mr. and Mrs. Harold X. Weinstein, 1961
Acq. no. 7.61
Ill. p. 55

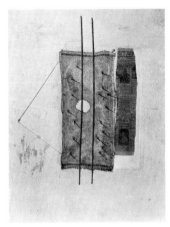

41. Picasso, *Guitar*, 1926. Estate of Pablo Picasso

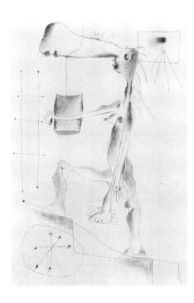

42. Drawing, 1937

43. Drawing, 1973. The Museum of Modern Art, New York

44. *Female Torso*, 1931. Louise and Walter Arensberg Collection, Philadelphia Museum of Art

45. Klee, *She Howls, We Play*, 1928. Paul Klee Foundation, Kunstmuseum, Bern

BATHER
Montroig, October 1932
Oil on wood, 14¾ x 18⅛ inches
Signed on reverse: "Joan Miró / 10–32 / 'Baigneuse'"
Provenance: Mr. and Mrs. Henry Clifford, Radnor, Pennsylvania; Sam Kootz, New York
Promised gift of Mr. and Mrs. Armand Bartos, New York
Ill. p. 57

1. Dupin (no. 324 and p. 250) puts this picture in the collection of the Wadsworth Atheneum, Hartford, Connecticut. It has, however, never been owned by that institution.

2. Dupin, p. 250.

3. It is not uncommon in Miró's work to find this kind of plastic *double entendre*. For another example, see discussion below, p. 82.

COLLAGE (Study for *Painting*, 1933)
Barcelona, February 11, 1933
Cut and pasted photomechanical reproductions and pencil, 18½ x 24⅞ inches
Inscribed lower left: "11.2.33 (195 x 173. 13.6.33.)"[1]
Acq. no. 131.73
Ill. p. 58

1. The first date (11.2.33) of this inscription indicates when the collage itself was executed, the second (13.6.33) is the date of the Museum's *Painting*, 1933 (p. 59), and the numbers 195 x 173 are the dimensions in centimeters of *Painting*.

PAINTING
Barcelona, (June 13, 1933)
Oil on canvas, 68½ x 77¼ inches
Provenance: Pierre Matisse Gallery, New York; George L. K. Morris, New York
Gift of the Advisory Committee (by exchange)
Acq. no. 229.37
Ill. p. 59

1. Almost all of the cutouts represent tools or parts of tools used in woodworking. The two largest are planers—possibly different views of the same machine equipped with a greater or lesser number of attachments. Likewise, the other images (with the possible exceptions of the gauge—middle left between the two main planers—and what may be an upside-down press in the middle of the lower right quadrant) are very likely components of the two largest machines.

2. Barr, *Masters of Modern Art*, p. 142; see also Soby, p. 70.

3. For discussion see the author's *Dada and Surrealist Art*, pp. 76–82.

4. Dupin, p. 252.

5. See p. 24 above.

DRAWING-COLLAGE
Montroig, August 8, 1933
Collage and charcoal drawing on green paper with 3 postcards,
  sandpaper, and 4 engravings, 42½ x 28⅜ inches
Signed on reverse: "Joan Miró / 8.8.33"
Provenance: The Donor, Woodbury, Connecticut
Kay Sage Tanguy Bequest
Acq. no. 328.63
Ill. p. 61

DRAWING-COLLAGE
Montroig, October 2, 1933
Charcoal and collage of cut and pasted photographs and offset
  reproduction, 25⅛ x 18⅝ inches
Signed on reverse: "Joan Miró / 2.10.33"
Provenance: Pierre Matisse Gallery, New York
Promised gift of an anonymous donor
Ill. p. 61

1. For discussion see the author's *Dada and Surrealist Art*, pp.
316, 326.

2. The projection formed by the large cartilage of the larynx
is described in the purest Spanish as *la nuez de la garganta*
(translated literally, "walnut of the throat"); however, the expression adopted from English, *la manzana de Adán* (literally,
"Adam's apple"), is also common.

3. "Les Plus Belles Cartes Postales," *Minotaure* (Paris), no. 3–4,
1933, pp. 85–100.

DRAWING-COLLAGE
(1933)
Charcoal, pencil, wash, and decal, 25¼ x 17⅛ inches
Signed lower center: "Miró"
Provenance: (Yvonne Zervos, Paris); The Donor, New York
Gift of Nelson A. Rockefeller
Acq. no. 194.56
Ill. p. 63

HIRONDELLE / AMOUR
(Winter 1933–34)
Oil on canvas, 6 feet 6½ inches x 8 feet 1½ inches
Inscribed center right: "hirondelle / amour"
Provenance: One of 4 cartoons for tapestries commissioned by
  Mme Marie Cuttoli, who, while she never owned the paint-
  ing, had it in her possession until 1946; Aimé Maeght, Paris
Promised Gift of Nelson A. Rockefeller, New York
Ill. p. 65

1. Although this work was previously cataloged and exhibited
as *L'Hirondelle d'Amour* ("The Swallow of Love"), Miró has
confirmed the author's assumption that, since neither the defi-
nite article nor the possessive *de* is actually written on the picture surface, the correct title of the picture is made up of the
two syntactically unrelated words "Hirondelle" and "Amour."

46. Ernst, *Loplop Introduces ...*, 1931. Ursula and Erno Goldfinger,
London

47. *Photo: Ceci est la couleur de mes rêves*, 1925. Private collection,
New York

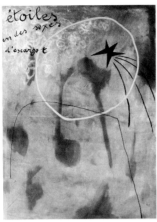

48. *Etoiles en des sexes d'escargot*, 1925. Kunstsammlung Nordrhein-Westfalen, Düsseldorf

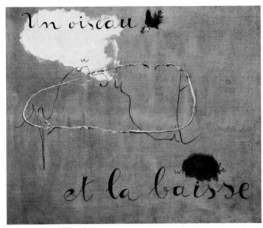

49. *Un Oiseau poursuit une abeille et la baisse*, 1927. Private collection, New York

50. *Musique, Seine, Michel, Bataille et moi*, 1927. Volkart Stiftung, Kunstmuseum, Winterthur, Switzerland

2. These four paintings were commissioned by Mme Marie Cuttoli, a well-known collector and an early patron of many of the major painters of this century. It is largely to her efforts that the French tapestry industry owes its revival after a decline of nearly two hundred years. Among other artists from whom she has commissioned tapestry cartoons are Matisse, Braque, and Picasso.

3. Among examples of Miró's picture-poems of the twenties are: *Photo: Ceci est la couleur de mes rêves*, 1925 (fig. 47 and Dupin, no. 125); *Etoiles en des sexes d'escargot*, 1925 (fig. 48 and Dupin, no. 108); *Un Oiseau poursuit une abeille et la baisse*, 1927 (fig. 49 and Dupin, no. 161); *Musique, Seine, Michel, Bataille et moi*, 1927 (fig. 50 and Dupin, no. 192). In these paintings, as in *Hirondelle / Amour*, the writing serves an essential plastic function within the pictorial structure while at the same time verbally reinforcing the emotional and connotative impact of the image. For an in-depth discussion of Miró's picture-poems see Krauss and Rowell, pp. 11–35, pp. 39–64 passim.

4. Pierre Schneider, "Miró," *Horizon* (New York), vol. 1, no. 4 (March 1959), p. 72.

COLLAGE
January 20, 1934
Collage on sandpaper, 14⅝ x 9⅜ inches
Signed on reverse: "Joan Miró / 20/1/34"
Promised gift of James Thrall Soby, New Canaan, Connecticut
Ill. p. 66

GOUACHE-DRAWING
August 1934
Gouache and pencil on paper, 42 x 28 inches
Signed on reverse: "Joan Miró / Août 1934 / 'Gouache-Dessin'"
Provenance: Pierre Matisse Gallery, New York
Promised gift of Mr. and Mrs. Gordon Bunshaft, New York
Ill. p. 67

OPERA SINGER
October 1934
Pastel, 41⅜ x 29⅛ inches
Signed on reverse: "Joan Miró / 'Femme' / Octobre 1934"
Provenance: Pierre Matisse Gallery, New York; The Donor, Westhampton Beach, New York
Gift of William H. Weintraub, 1964
Acq. no. 509.64
Ill. p. 68

ROPE AND PEOPLE I
March 27, 1935
Oil on cardboard mounted on wood, with coil of rope,
 41¼ x 29⅜ inches
Signed on wooden backing: "Joan Miró / 'Corde et
 personnages.' / 27-3-35"
Gift of the Pierre Matisse Gallery, 1936
Acq. no. 71.36
Ill. p. 69

OBJECT
Barcelona, (spring 1936)
Construction of hollowed wooden post, stuffed parrot on
 wooden stand, hat, and map, 31⅞ inches high x 11⅞ inches
 wide x 10¼ inches deep
Signed bottom of parrot's stand: "miró"
Provenance: Mrs. Kenneth F. Simpson, New York;
 The Donors, New York
Gift of Mr. and Mrs. Pierre Matisse, 1965
Acq. no. 940.65 a-c
Ill. p. 71

51. Duchamp, *Why Not Sneeze?* (1964 replica of 1921 original).
The Museum of Modern Art, New York

1. For discussion see the author's *Dada and Surrealist Art*, pp.
36–43.

2. Marcel Duchamp in a round-table discussion, "The Art of
Assemblage," at The Museum of Modern Art, New York,
October 19, 1961. Other participants were William C. Seitz
(moderator), Lawrence Alloway, Richard Huelsenbeck, Robert Rauschenberg, and Roger Shattuck.

3. André Breton, *Introduction au discours sur le peu de réalité*
(Paris: Gallimard, 1927), p. 33.

4. See the author's "The Surrealism of the Thirties," in *Dada
and Surrealist Art*, pp. 210–78, especially pp. 211, 249.

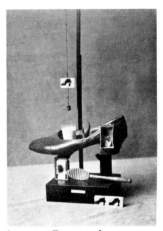

52. Dali, *Object of Symbolic Function*, 1931. Destroyed

5. Although the original map is owned by the Museum, it is
badly deteriorated and has been replaced with a map, approved and signed by Miró, that is as close to the original in
appearance as possible.

6. Dali, in "Objets surréalistes," *Le Surréalisme au Service de la
Révolution* (Paris), no. 3 (December 1931), p. 17, describes
his *Object of Symbolic Function* as "A woman's shoe, inside
of which has been placed a cup of lukewarm milk [resting] in
the middle of paste of ductile form and excremental color.
The mechanism consists of lowering a piece of sugar, on which
has been painted the image of a shoe, in order to observe its
dissolution—and consequently [that of] the image of the
shoe—[during its immersion] in the milk. Many accessories
(pubic hairs glued to a sugar cube, a small erotic photo) complete the object, which is accompanied by a reserve box of
sugar and a special spoon that serves to stir the lead pellets inside the shoe."

7. Maurice Nadeau, in *Histoire du surréalisme*, 2nd ed. (Paris:
Club des Editeurs, 1958), p. 176, reports: "Everyone who saw
this object functioning experienced a strong but indefinable
sexual emotion relating to unconscious desires. This emotion

53. Giacometti, *Suspended Ball*, 1930–31

was in no sense one of satisfaction, but one of disturbance, like that imparted by the irritating awareness of failure."

8. While the metamorphic birds in Miró's paintings never strictly resemble any particular species, the bird that "deciphers the unknown to a pair of lovers" in the Museum's *Constellation* (p. 80) has a distinctly parrotlike head. It is not impossible that Miró's choice of a parrot in this object identifies it as "the bird of love"—or is related to the deciphering or decoding of the sculpture's enigma.

AIDEZ L'ESPAGNE
1937
Stencil, printed in color (from *Cahiers d'Art*, vol. 12, no. 4–5, 1937), 9¾ x 7⅝ inches
Signed and inscribed in collotype, bottom margin of sheet: "Dans la lutte actuelle, je vois du côté fasciste les forces périmées, de l'autre côté le peuple dont les immenses ressources créatrices donneront à l'Espagne un élan qui étonnera le monde. / Miró"
Gift of Pierre Matisse, 1949
Acq. no. 634.49
Ill. p. 72

STILL LIFE WITH OLD SHOE
Paris, January 24–May 29, 1937
Oil on canvas, 32¼ x 46 inches
Signed on stretcher: "Joan Miró / Nature Morte au Vieux Soulier / 24-1-29-v. 1937"
Provenance: Pierre Matisse Gallery, New York; Mr. and Mrs. Earle Miller, Downington, Pennsylvania; Pierre Matisse Gallery, New York; The Donor, New Canaan, Connecticut
Fractional gift of James Thrall Soby
Acq. no. 1094.69
Ill. p. 73

1. Dupin, p. 293.

2. Penrose, *Miró*, p. 86.

3. Jacques Lassaigne, *Miró*, trans. Stuart Gilbert (Geneva: Skira, 1963), p. 77.

4. Soby, p. 149, reports, "This object has been identified by Miró himself as an apple, not a potato or squash."

5. Soby, p. 80.

6. First observed by James Johnson Sweeney, in *Joan Miró* (The Museum of Modern Art), p. 68.

7. This point has been made by Meyer Schapiro in lectures at Columbia University and is summarized in his book *Vincent van Gogh* (New York: Harry N. Abrams, 1950), pp. 28, 32.

54. *The Reaper*. Mural, now lost, painted for the pavilion of the Spanish Republic at the Paris World's Fair, 1937

55. *Self-Portrait*, 1938–60. Sra. Pilar Juncosa de Miró, Palma

HEAD OF A MAN
Montroig, (summer 1937)
Gouache and India ink on black paper, 25⅝ x 19¾ inches
Signed lower right center: "Miró"
Provenance: Pierre Matisse Gallery, New York
Promised gift of an anonymous donor
Ill. p. 75

SELF-PORTRAIT I
Paris, 1937–38
Pencil, crayon, and oil on canvas, 57½ x 38¼ inches
Signed upper right: "Miró"; and on reverse: "Joan Miró /
    Autoportrait I / 1937–1938"
Provenance: Pierre Matisse, New York
Promised gift of James Thrall Soby, New Canaan,
    Connecticut
Ill. p. 77

1. Sweeney, *Joan Miró* (The Museum of Modern Art), p. 70.

2. Soby, p. 93.

3. Dupin, p. 303.

4. In 1960 or shortly thereafter, he painted over a facsimile of the *Self-Portrait* with heavy graffitilike contours and flat colors (fig. 55), much in the manner he has painted over the pictures of other artists, as instanced by *Portrait of a Man in a Late Nineteenth Century Frame* (p. 84). There are conflicting accounts of when this facsimile was executed. In *Joan Miró*, published in 1959, Soby states (p. 93): "When the portrait was completed he [Miró] decided to try his hand at a second and much more colorful version. He therefore traced the composition on another canvas of the same size and pondered the problem of strengthening the tonal brilliance. He quickly came to the conclusion that the original version was complete in itself, and the tracing was abandoned, though a photograph of it has survived and been published" (fig. 56, photo reproduced in *Joan Miró*, Images de Roger Hauert, Texte d'André Verdet [Geneva: Editions René Kister, 1956]). Two years later, however, in a letter (in the files of The Museum of Modern Art) to Dorothy Miller and Alfred Barr dated March 8, 1961, he says: "Pierre [Matisse] had told me that the second version was a tracing made by Miró himself after the first version was finished. This puzzled me, since I couldn't understand how even a tracing by Miró could seem so hard and mechanical. I couldn't see how Miró could have done it. He didn't. This week at luncheon Miró told me that the tracing was made by one Fries or Friez . . . who was a draftsman in the office of Paul Nelson in one of whose buildings Miró lived in Paris when he did the original version of the self portrait. The tracing was apparently made as a sort of record for Miró to keep. It was stored in Paris for years and then, around 1960 Miró painted a head in very heavy contours over it, as he has sometimes done over earlier portraits by other artists." Dupin in 1962 (p. 484 of his book) says, "Miró recently had a copy made of the work," and Penrose in 1969 (*Miró*, p. 97) states:

56. Miró with facsimile self-portrait, c. 1956. Photo by Roger Hauert, courtesy of Editions Kister, Geneva

57. Miró and Marcoussis, *Portrait of Miró*, 1938. The Museum of Modern Art, New York

58. *Self-Portrait*, 1919. Estate of Pablo Picasso

59. *Self-Portrait II*, 1938. The Detroit Institute of Arts, Gift of W. Hawkins Ferry

60. *Seated Woman II*, 1939. Peggy Guggenheim Foundation, Venice

61. *Object of Sunset*, 1938. Estate of André Breton

"More than twenty years later, in 1960, he again took up the same theme. After installing himself in his new studio in Majorca, he unpacked a large number of pre-war paintings and found himself in contemplation of the past. He had an exact copy in black and white made of the first self-portrait of 1937, with the intention of working on it with the detailed precision of a Mantegna." On the basis of Soby's 1961 account and the photograph published in 1956, it seems most logical that the copy was executed shortly after *Self-Portrait I*. There is, in addition to the facsimile, an etching after *Self-Portrait* done in 1938 by Miró and Marcoussis (fig. 57), both of whom worked on the plate. The print (in an edition of fifty) is in no sense an exact copy of the painting, although clearly inspired by it. Inscribed in the plate is "pluie de lyres / cirques de mélancolie."

5. Soby, p. 93.

6. See Sweeney, "Miró," *Art News Annual*, p. 68.

7. Dupin, p. 304.

SEATED WOMAN I
Paris, December 24, 1938
Oil on canvas, 64⅜ x 51⅝ inches
Signed upper right: "Miró"; and on reverse: "JOAN MIRO / Femme assise I / 24/12/1938"
Provenance: Pierre Matisse Gallery, New York; The Donors, Westhampton Beach, New York
Fractional gift of Mr. and Mrs. William H. Weintraub
Acq. no. 1532.68
Ill. p. 79

1. To avoid confusion, it should be pointed out that Dupin (nos. 517, 518 and pp. 312, 345) has reversed the chronology of the two versions of *Seated Woman*, cataloging the Museum's picture as *Seated Woman II* and the one in the Peggy Guggenheim Collection (fig. 60) as *Seated Woman I*. The dates he gives for the two pictures are in error; the Museum's picture is dated as above, and the Guggenheim painting is dated February 27, 1939.

2. Although less tightly rendered, this form is virtually the same as that of the sun in *The Hunter* (p. 23), and its dual function as solar sign and sexual symbol is discussed p. 24 above. It is also interesting to compare this sex-sun with that of Miró's *Object of Sunset* (fig. 61), executed in the same year.

THE BEAUTIFUL BIRD REVEALING THE UNKNOWN TO A
PAIR OF LOVERS
Montroig, July 23, 1941
Gouache and oil wash, 18 x 15 inches
Signed left of center bottom: "miró"; inscribed on reverse
  within a design: "Joan Miró / Le bel oiseau déchiffrant
  l'inconnu / au couple d'amoureux / montroig / 23/VII/1941'
Provenance: Pierre Matisse Gallery, New York
Acquired through the Lillie P. Bliss Bequest, 1945
Acq. no. 7.45
Ill. p. 80

1. The literal translation of the French title that Miró inscribed on the reverse of this picture is: "The Beautiful Bird
Deciphering the Unknown to the Pair of Lovers." Because this
rendering loses something of the poetry of the original, "revealing" has traditionally been used instead of "deciphering."
Nonetheless, the implications of the latter word should not be
lost, for they introduce the idea of ciphers, and hence numbers
and decoding, important both to the character of the configuration and the complexities of the reading.

2. André Breton, "Constellations de Joan Miró," *L'Oeil* (Paris),
no. 48 (December 1958), p. 51.

3. Dupin, p. 357.

4. Sweeney, "Comment and Interview," p. 211.

5. Ibid.

6. The so-called "hourglass" form itself reads as a variant of
the circle (also repeated all over the surface) in that it is
formed by the intersection of two diameters and thus implies
the full round or oval.

7. Penrose, *Miró*, p. 104.

8. Dupin, p. 358.

9. Sweeney, "Comment and Interview," p. 210.

PAINTING
1950
Oil on canvas, 32 x 39½ inches
Signed on reverse: "Miró / 1950"
Provenance: Pierre Matisse Gallery, New York
Promised gift of Mr. and Mrs. Gordon Bunshaft, New York
Ill. p. 83

PORTRAIT OF A MAN IN A LATE NINETEENTH CENTURY FRAME
1950
Oil on canvas with ornamented wood frame, 57½ x 49¼
  inches (including frame)
Signed on reverse: "Miró / 1950"
Provenance: Mr. and Mrs. Pierre Matisse, New York
Gift of Pierre Matisse, 1972
Acq. no. 210.72
Ill. p. 84

1. The title was given to the picture by Miró (see Sweeney,
"Miró" [*Art News Annual*], p. 81), and although the frame
may in fact date from sometime shortly-after 1900, its heavy
ornamentation is characteristic of a kind of bourgeois, humor-
less, decorative style prevalent in the latter part of the last century. The title also certainly expresses Miró's vision of the
sitter, whose life has been delimited within the "frame" of the
nineteenth-century bourgeois mentality.

2. As noted in catalog entry, the work has been dated 1950 by
Miró. There are, however, notations on the stretcher giving
other dates: 1945 crossed out to read 1949; 1950 crossed out to
read 1949. Sweeney, "Miró" (*Art News Annual*), p. 81, dates
it 1945.

62. *Study for the Harkness Commons Dining Room Mural*, 1950. Fogg Art Museum, Cambridge, Massachusetts

63. *Mural Painting* as installed in Harkness Commons Dining Room, c. 1951

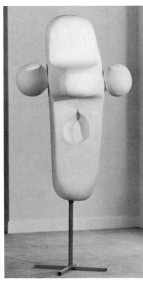

64. *Tête de femme*, 1970. Galerie Maeght, Paris

MURAL PAINTING
Barcelona, (1950–51)
Oil on canvas, 6 feet 2¾ inches x 19 feet 5¾ inches
Signed lower left: "Miró"
Provenance: Harvard University, Cambridge, Massachusetts;
  Pierre Matisse Gallery, New York
Mrs. Simon Guggenheim Fund, 1963
Acq. no. 592.63
Ill. p. 86, foldout

1. Questionnaire in the files of The Museum of Modern Art dated March 16, 1964.

2. Ibid.

3. Ibid.

4. Dupin, p. 430.

5. This reading was suggested by Margit Rowell of the Guggenheim Museum. It is especially interesting since the preparatory sketch seems to support the theory.

6. Soby, p. 126, speaks of "the protruding head at the left of the sketch."

XXIII from *Barcelona Series*
1944
Lithograph, 24⅜ x 18⁹⁄₁₆ inches
1/5
Purchase, 1945
Acq. no. 134.45
Ill. p. 88

XLVII from *Barcelona Series*
1944
Lithograph, 10 x 13 inches
1/5
Purchase, 1945
Acq. no. 135.45
Ill. p. 89

PERSONAGE
Barcelona, (1947)
Ceramic, 32½ inches high
Signed on back: "Miró / Artigas"
Provenance: Galerie Maeght, Paris; H. Uhlman, Paris;
  Galerie du Dragon, Paris
Promised gift of Mr. and Mrs. Edwin A. Bergman, Chicago
Ill. p. 90

HEAD
Gallifa, (1954)
Ceramic, 9½ x 18 inches
Signed on back: "Miró / Artigas"
Provenance: Pierre Matisse Gallery, New York
Promised gift of an anonymous donor
Ill. p. 91

CONCRETE WRITING (Graphisme concret)
1953
Charcoal, brush, and ink, 19⅜ x 25⅛ inches
Signed on reverse: "Miró / 1953 / Graphisme concret"
Provenance: Pierre Matisse Gallery, New York;
 Frumkin Gallery, New York
Extended loan of the Joan and Lester Avnet Collection
E.L. 70.710
Ill. p. 92

PERSON, WOMAN, BIRD, STAR AT SUNSET
1953
Oil and gesso on gouged and burnt composition board,
 42½ x 21½ inches
Signed middle right, near edge: "Miró"; dated on reverse:
 "1953"
Provenance: Pierre Matisse Gallery, New York;
 G. David Thompson, Pittsburgh
Kay Sage Tanguy Fund, 1966
Acq. no. 198.66
Ill. p. 93

SERIES I, PLATE IV (*The Family*)
1952
Etching, engraving, and aquatint, printed in color,
 14¹⁵⁄₁₆ x 17⅞ inches
8/13
Curt Valentin Bequest, 1955
Acq. no. 355.55
Ill. p. 94

EQUINOX
1968
Etching and aquatint, printed in color, 41¹⁄₁₆ x 29 inches
Gift of Studebaker-Worthington, Inc., 1973
Acq. no. 177.73
Ill. p. 95

THE SONG OF THE VOWELS
Palma, April 24, 1966
Oil on canvas, 12 feet ⅛ inch x 45¼ inches
Signed and dated on reverse: "MIRO / 24/IV /66/
 LA CHANSON DES VOYELLES"
Provenance: Pierre Matisse Gallery, New York
Mrs. Simon Guggenheim Fund, special contribution in honor
 of Dorothy C. Miller, 1970
Acq. no. 57.70
Ill. p. 97

1. The reference here is to such "allover" works as the early
paintings of Larry Poons. These, however, are immediately
indebted to the plus-and-minus Mondrian and the allover Pollock and are executed for the most part with the tightness of
hard-edge painting. Nevertheless it is significant that Poons
arrived at his style through an effort to directly translate the
effects of musical notation into a pictorial format.

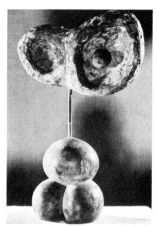

65. *Female Torso*, 1967. Pierre Matisse Gallery, New York

66. *The Writer*, 1924. Pierre Janlet, Brussels

67. *Bird*, 1944. Fondation Maeght, St-Paul, A. M., France

68. *Sunbird*, 1966. The Art Institute of Chicago, Grant J. Pick Fund

69. *Bird*, 1944. Fondation Maeght, St-Paul, A. M., France

MOONBIRD
(1966)
Bronze, 7 feet 8⅛ inches x 6 feet 9¼ inches x 59⅛ inches
Incised back of right leg: "Miró / EPREUVE D'ARTISTE I / III";
and back of left leg, "SUSSE FONDEUR. PARIS"
Acquired through the Lillie P. Bliss Bequest, 1970
Acq. no. 515.70
Ill. p. 99

1. Cited by Dean Swanson in "The Artist's Comments / Extracts from an Interview with Joan Miró (19 August 1970, St-Paul-de-Vence)," *Miró Sculptures*, catalog of an exhibition organized by the Walker Art Center, Minneapolis, October 3–November 28, 1971.

2. *Sunbird* of 1966 (fig. 68), the piece with which *Moonbird* is "paired," also derives from a small work of 1944 (fig. 69). According to David Sylvester ("About Miró's Sculpture," *Miró Bronzes*, Arts Council of Great Britain, Hayward Gallery, February 1–March 12, 1972, p. 9 of the catalog), these birds were the first pieces Miró completed when he began working in clay "on his own" (without the collaboration of Artigas).

3. "Pointing-up" is a technique for producing an enlarged, exact-scale version of a sculpture. Many of Arp's large bronzes were "pointed-up" from smaller pieces, often in plaster.

4. Sylvester, p. 15.

5. Notable exceptions to this treatment of sex occur throughout the group of pictures called by Miró his *tableaux sauvages* (see p. 68), as well as numerous drawings of the mid-thirties (see p. 68 and fig. 42), particularly those executed from life at the Académie de la Grande Chaumière in 1937 just before the execution of *Still Life with Old Shoe*.

PERSONAGE AND BIRD
Palma, (1968)
Bronze; cast number two of an edition of two,
  41 x 25¼ x 7⅛ inches
Provenance: Pierre Matisse Gallery, New York
Promised gift of Mr. and Mrs. Gordon Bunshaft, New York
Ill. p. 101

1. Cited by Swanson, n.p.

2. See, for example, *Seated Woman and Child* and *Head and
Bird*. These pieces are illustrated in color in Swanson, catalog
nos. 15 and 17.

3. John Russell, *Miró*, New York, Pierre Matisse Gallery, May
1970, n.p.

WOMAN WITH THREE HAIRS SURROUNDED BY
  BIRDS IN THE NIGHT
Palma, September 2,[2] 1972
Oil on canvas, 95⅞ x 66½ inches
Signed lower left: "Miró"; and on reverse: "MIRO / 2/IX/72"
Gift of the artist in honor of James Thrall Soby, 1973
Acq. no. 116.73
Ill. p. 103

1. Miró's small *Bird* of 1944 (fig. 69) might be considered as
being directly derived from a characteristic type (fig. 71) of
Majorcan folk sculpture.

2. This date, inscribed on the canvas, marks the day the picture
was completed. The actual process of painting it went on over
a period of weeks as outlined in the text above.

SOBRETEIXIM 5
Palma, May 1, 1972
Painted rope, wool, and wire mesh on hemp woven ground,
  64 x 68 inches
Signed on reverse on sewn-on label: "Sobreteixim
  5 / 1/v/9.72 / Miró"
Provenance: Pierre Matisse Gallery, New York
Promised gift of Mr. and Mrs. Gordon Bunshaft
Ill. p. 104

70. "The Matron," folk sculpture, Majorca

71. Folk sculpture, Majorca

LIST OF REFERENCE ILLUSTRATIONS

Picasso. *Three Dancers*. 1925. (fig. 29, p. 118)

Raphael, attributed to. *La Fornarina*. (fig. 37, p. 121)

Redon. *The Eye Like a Strange Balloon Mounts toward Infinity*. 1882. (fig. 8, p. 112)

Sorgh. Colored postcard of *The Lutanist* by Hendrick Maertensz Sorgh. (p. 40)

Tzara, Hugo, Knutsen, Breton. *Cadavre exquis*. c. 1926. (fig. 31, p. 118)

Fragment from the apse of Sant Climent de Taull. (fig. 7, p. 112)

"The Deluge," from the *Apocalypse of Saint-Sever*. (fig. 17, p. 115)

Folk sculpture. Majorca. (fig. 71, p. 135)

"The Matron." Folk sculpture. Majorca. (fig. 70, p. 135)

Miró with facsimile self-portrait. c. 1956. (fig. 56, p. 129)